Attracting BIRDS, BUTTERFLIES & Other WINGED WONDERS to Your BACKYARD

Attracting BIRDS, BUTTERFLIES & Other WINGED WONDERS to Your BACKYARD

Kris Wetherbee

PHOTOGRAPHY:
RICK WETHERBEE

LARK BOOKS

A Division of Sterling
Publishing Co., Inc.
New York

To my dad & mom,
Ed & Alice Reed,
who started me on
my journey with nature.

EDITOR: JANE HARRIS WOODSIDE

ART DIRECTOR: SUSAN MCBRIDE

PHOTOGRAPHER: RICK WETHERBEE

COVER DESIGNER: BARBARA ZARETSKY

TECHNICAL ILLUSTRATOR: ORRIN LUNDGREN

GARDEN PLAN ILLUSTRATOR: SUSAN MCBRIDE

EDITORIAL ASSISTANCE: DELORES GOSNELL,
REBECCA GUTHRIE, SUSAN KIEFFER,
NATHALIE MORNU, TERRY KRAUTWURST,
VALERIE SHRADER

ASSOCIATE ART DIRECTOR: SHANNON YOKELEY

EDITORIAL INTERNS: JANNA NORTON,
MATTHEW PADEN

SPECIAL PHOTOGRAPHY:
RON AUSTING, PAINTED BUNTING, PAGE 135;
BLUE JAYS, PAGE 140; EASTERN TOWEE,
PAGE 145.

SCOTT BAUER, ARS/USDA, ORCHARD MASON
BEE, PAGE 109.

GLENN CORBIERE, FAMILIAR BLUET, PAGE 158;
SPOTTED SPREADWINGS, PAGE 159; BLUE
DASHER, PAGE 160; SHADOW DARNER, PAGE
161; AUTUMN MEADOWHAWK, PAGE 162.

PAUL A. OPLER, MOURNING CLOAK AND
AMERICAN PAINTED LADY, PAGE 149.

D. LYNN SCOTT, POLYPHEMUS, PAGE 155;
VIRGIN TIGER, PAGE 156; ILIA, PAGE 157.

COVER PHOTOGRAPHY: RICK WETHERBEE

Library of Congress Cataloging-in-Publication Data

Wetherbee, Kris.
  Attracting birds, butterflies & other winged wonders to your backyard / by
Kris Wetherbee.-- 1st ed.
    p. cm.
  Includes index.
  ISBN 1-57990-594-3 (hardcover)
  1. Bird attracting. 2. Butterfly attracting. I. Title. II. Title:
Attracting birds, butterflies and other winged wonders to your backyard.
QL676.5.W44 2005
598'.072'34--dc22

                    2004025160

10 9 8 7 6 5 4 3 2 1

First Edition

Published by Lark Books, A division of
Sterling Publishing Co., Inc.
387 Park Avenue South, New York, N.Y. 10016

Text © 2004, Kris Wetherbee
Project designs © 2004, Kris and Rick Wetherbee
Photography © 2004, Rick Wetherbee
Illustrations © 2004, Lark Books

Distributed in Canada by Sterling Publishing,
c/o Canadian Manda Group, 165 Dufferin Street
Toronto, Ontario, Canada M6K 3H6

Distributed in the U.K. by Guild of Master Craftsman Publications Ltd., Castle
Place, 166 High Street, Lewes, East Sussex, England BN7 1XU
Tel: (+ 44) 1273 477374, Fax: (+ 44) 1273 478606,
e-mail: pubs@thegmcgroup.com, Web: www.gmcpublications.com

Distributed in Australia by Capricorn Link (Australia) Pty Ltd.,
P.O. Box 704, Windsor, NSW 2756 Australia

The written instructions, photographs, designs, patterns, and projects in this volume are intended for the personal use of the reader and may be reproduced for that purpose only. Any other use, especially commercial use, is forbidden under law without written permission of the copyright holder.

Every effort has been made to ensure that all the information in this book is accurate. However, due to differing conditions, tools, and individual skills, the publisher cannot be responsible for any injuries, losses, and other damages that may result from the use of the information in this book.

For information about custom editions, special sales, premium and corporate purchases, please contact Sterling Special Sales Department at 800-805-5489 or specialsales@sterlingpub.com.

If you have questions or comments about this book,
please contact:
Lark Books
67 Broadway
Asheville, NC 28801
(828) 253-0467

Manufactured in China

ISBN 1-57990-594-3

Contents

INTRODUCTION

A tree swallow feeds her young nestled inside one of our many birdhouses.

Gulf fritillary butterfly

Whenever I step outside my front door, I cross the threshold into a wonderland where birds, butterflies, and other winged creatures come to visit, and many often stay. That wasn't always the case. Nearly 15 years ago, the landscape surrounding our house in western Oregon consisted mostly of weedy ground and barren soil in back, with a wide expanse of gravel in front. Though some shrubs, conifers, and evergreen trees surrounded the area, few birds or butterflies ventured within viewing distance of our home.

Since that time my husband, Rick, and I have planted several gardens that have grown into a naturescape of fruit-bearing trees and shrubs, along with plenty of perennials and annuals. More than two dozen birdhouses surround our kitchen garden in back, and each spring, the swallows and bluebirds return to nest, producing yet another generation for us to enjoy. In spring and summer, the front courtyard becomes a butterfly magnet, frequented by many species, including the western tiger swallowtail, painted lady, and my childhood favorite,

the ever sociable skipper. Even in the dead of winter, resident nuthatches, juncos, and other songbirds take refuge in the garden while feasting on seedheads from spent flowers, winterberries, or their favorite seed from one of the feeders. With each new season, we discover that more and more species of birds as well as butterflies, moths, dragonflies, and other beneficial bugs are enjoying our gardens. Their presence enhances our lives and gives us enormous pleasure throughout the year.

WHAT'S AHEAD

This book reflects my experience with and enthusiasm for attracting winged wildlife. Here you'll find all the information you need to create a beautiful and successful natural habitat, whether you want to turn a corner of your yard into a butterfly refuge, create a fragrant night-blooming moth sanctuary, or transform your entire property into a symphonic songbird garden. There's plenty of material about choosing trees, shrubs, ground covers, perennials, and annuals, including specifics about how to phase-in your naturescaping and incorporate water features. You can start small—by adding a few trees and plants, accented with bird feeders, nest boxes, birdbaths, and simple but attractive

Dahlias and crocosmia border a bark-covered path through a garden of perennials, shrubs, and trees—all the right elements for attracting birds, butterflies, and other winged wildlife.

shelters for beneficial insects. Although garden supply stores carry all kinds of bird feeders, why not make your own? Instructions are provided for building more than 20 great-looking projects: for example, feeders to attract both birds and butterflies, nest boxes, a dragonfly perch, orchard bee nests—even a beneficial bug bath. Plus you'll find information in the profiles about how to attract specific kinds of winged wildlife. Throughout the book, there are also dozens of interesting tidbits and fascinating facts to help you enjoy your new neighbors.

MAKING A WILDLIFE WISH LIST

If you want to attract winged wildlife to your own yard, the first question you need to answer is: which wildlife species can you attract? After all, it's fruitless to install a purple martin house if there are no purple martins to be found in your corner of the country. A good place to start is to check the wildlife profiles located at the end of this book. These profiles furnish descriptions, ranges, and tips about how to attract many species of birds, butterflies, moths, dragonflies, and damselflies. Once you've determined which species live in your vicinity, you can design your wildlife habitat either to entice a particular group—hummingbirds or swallows, for example—or to invite a variety of species to take up residence right outside your door.

You'll also need to decide just how large a wildlife habitat you're ready and willing to create. A wildlife-friendly garden doesn't need to be large to do the job. With careful planning, you can increase the winged population of your yard noticeably with a habitat covering as little as, say, 10 x 10 feet if you already have existing trees and shrubs (or one that measures 300 square feet—30 by 10 feet, for example—if you're starting from scratch). Of course, the larger the habitat the greater the rewards—we can attest that after transforming our 3,000-square-foot yard into a garden that welcomes wildlife. You might well find yourself starting small and then being inspired to add on over the years.

The perennial patch of flowers in this wildlife garden includes purple coneflower, blanket flowers, and zinnias—plants that provide nectar for hummingbirds, butterflies, and beneficial insects, as well as seeds for birds.

An American robin perched on a grape vine growing over an arbor

BASIC NEEDS

No matter what size garden you have in mind, you need to remember the basic secret to creating a habitat welcoming to wildlife. Simply put, the creature comforts that make your yard a more nature-friendly place are the same ones we all need for survival: food, fresh water, protective cover, and a cozy shelter.

Food preferences vary, depending of course on the particular species and also, at times, on the location, and time of year. In addition to insects and worms, different types of winged wildlife and their offspring need seeds, leaves, nuts, nectar, fruits, berries, and even tree sap for fuel. Growing trees, shrubs, ground covers, and flowers that produce food in summer will certainly entice winged creatures to come for a visit. However, they'll be more likely to stay awhile—and perhaps even nest—when there's an abundance of food available throughout each of the four seasons.

When the weather outside is frightful, shelter is what delights wildlife the most. Dense deciduous trees and shrubs as well as evergreens provide not only a much needed refuge from the elements—such as a sudden downpour, pounding hail, a blizzard, or searing heat—but also protection from predators and a safe place to breed or just rest for the night. Then there are the grasses, low-growing conifers, and trailing blackberries that create a sanctuary for ground-nesting birds, a windfall of insects for ground-feeders, and places for dragonflies to perch. Even vines, such as Virginia creeper or honeysuckle, offer a place where birds, butterflies, and moths can perch and nest.

Some dragonfly species, such as the female widow skimmer shown perched on a verbena, venture away from water.

A clean, accessible, year-round water source is a necessity that's easily overlooked—yet it is often more scarce than food in many urban and suburban landscapes. Always indispensable in especially hot or dry areas, wildlife water sources are extremely crucial during the summer. A small pond or pool is always ideal, but even a rudimentary birdbath can meet birds' needs for a place to drink and bathe. Of course it's not just birds that need water. If you meet wildlife's basic need for water, you'll be guaranteed to attract a wide variety of butterflies and beneficial bugs, too. Once they've discovered a source of water in your backyard, many will keep coming back—much to your delight as well as theirs.

Many species of birds have taken advantage of the birdbath in our large backyard garden. On this particular late spring afternoon, a male purple finch came to visit.

Whether in full bloom or not, this wildlife haven is as beautiful as it is functional. Rhododendrons, azaleas, and flowering dogwood provide a complete package of food, shelter, and nesting sites for a variety of winged creatures.

Clipper butterfly

KEY PRINCIPLES: DIVERSITY & WILDLIFE ZONING

Diversity is key. Whether in a small- or large-scale garden, it's important to have the right mix of plants—trees, shrubs, ground covers, vines, and flowers—in addition to amenities such as feeders, birdhouses, and baths. Together, they provide a complete package of food, shelter, and water for wildlife. And you'll not only be rewarded each and every day with the chance to observe wildlife up close, but you'll have the satisfaction of knowing you're helping to combat habitat loss, the leading cause of wildlife population decline.

Once you've created a welcoming place for winged wildlife, you'll find that gardening becomes more enjoyable and, perhaps, a bit easier too. That's because a fascinating synergy exists between the garden and nature's winged creatures. For starters, birds, butterflies, and beneficial bugs assist in the regeneration of plants: birds disperse the seeds of everything from lowly ground covers to stately trees while butterflies and beneficial bugs such as nonstinging bees lend a hand in pollination. And birds and beneficial bugs are among the most effective natural forms of controlling pest insects that damage or even kill plants. Over her lifetime,

This woodland wildlife garden features a diversity of plants at all levels—from ground covers and vines to towering trees. Birds especially appreciate the birdhouses located beneath the shelter of this large tree.

for example, a lady beetle can eat on the order of 2,500 aphids, pests that can damage roses, vegetables, trees, and shrubs.

As you devise your planting strategy on whatever scale you choose, always remember to think vertically as well as horizontally. Wildlife habitats exist at various levels of the vertical space that exists between the canopy and the soil. The uppermost tree branches form the canopy, or highest level. Smaller trees, shrubs, and vines compose the understory while just below lies the lower horizon, featuring low-growing shrubs, perennials, and annuals. Finally ground covers—which offer habitats for soil-dwelling crea-

tures, beetles, and ground-feeding birds—blanket the floor. By grouping your plants in layers, or wildlife zones, you can cater to different species of wildlife, whether they feed or nest on the ground, in trees and bushes, or in the air.

I trust this book will lead you on a marvelous gardening and wildlife adventure. Once you begin transforming your yard and seeing the results unfold, you'll have an intimate look at wildlife that's bound to be one of the most rewarding experiences of your life.

Chapter 1

STARTING SMALL

Sometimes big things really do come wrapped up in small packages. At least they do in the wildlife garden, where small-scale attractions can lead to large-scale delights for birds, butterflies, and other creatures that fly. There are lots of ways to attract winged wildlife with simple steps and small projects.

For example, have you ever thought about the fact that when it comes to wildlife, a brush pile has the potential to be so much more than just a place to toss unwanted branches? If you take just a little extra care, you can construct your pile so it becomes a place where dragonflies will perch, birds like wrens can find a ready source of the insects they crave, and other birds such as juncos and

sparrows will build their nests in the secure, sheltered spots they favor. Provide a container or two filled with dust, and you'll be able to watch birds taking a dust bath. Or set out a few stones, and be treated to the sight of butterflies basking in the sun. Scattered throughout this book are brief Fast Track features that give you specific instructions on how to do these simple but effective projects.

You can also purchase various feeders, shelters, and water sources that will catch the attention of wildlife of all kinds and draw them to your yard. But it's so much more rewarding to make these amenities yourself. In this chapter, as well as in chapters 5 through 7, you'll find plenty of projects that both attract wildlife and are pleasing additions to your landscape. And finally, if you choose plantings armed with the knowledge about what they can do for wildlife, you'll see results. The plant lists in chapters 3 and 4, plus the wildlife profiles in chapter 9, will give you what you need to make those informed choices. For instance, you'll see an increase in your butterfly population if you simply plant a butterfly bush or follow the suggestions in this chapter for container plantings or window boxes. All of these simple steps take little time or space.

Geraniums, easily grown in containers, are a great way to lure butterflies and hummingbirds, such as the female rufous hummingbird seen here. Place the containers on a deck or patio so you can enjoy them up close.

DID YOU KNOW?

While one hummingbird can visit hundreds of flowers a day, a hummer's diet doesn't just consist of nectar-rich flowers. They also consume protein-packed spiders and a variety of small insects snatched from a spider's web, from flowers, or from the sky.

Container PLANTINGS

Imagine the excitement of seeing a hummingbird by your kitchen window as it hovers in midair, sipping sweet nectar from a hanging basket brimming with colorful fuchsias, trailing lantana, or cascading geraniums. Window box gardens filled with nectar favorites like verbena, dianthus, penstemon, and daisies are a delightful way to attract butterflies, hummingbirds, and moths to a balcony, patio, veranda, or deck. Want to attract songbirds? Use containers to grow plants that have an abundance of seeds that are attractive to birds, plants such as rudbeckia, coreopsis, globe thistle, or sedums. And don't forget robins, waxwings, orioles, and other birds that feast on fruits and berries. They will particularly enjoy the berries of roses, hollies, cotoneaster, and even junipers—again, all easily grown in large containers.

With few exceptions, just about any plant, shrub, vine, or small tree that attracts wildlife can be grown in a container. Whether in the form of planters, hanging baskets, or window box gardens, container plantings are a quick and compact way to dish up a portable feast for winged wildlife. And you can prepare that feast year-round. Grow food sources that are available from season to season: annual phlox, calendula, and primrose for spring bloom; geraniums, sunflowers, and petunias for summer sensations; asters, salvia, and ornamental grasses for autumn

Dress up a deck with color and attract hummingbirds, butterflies, and various beneficial insects by choosing wildlife-friendly plants, like the petunias and verbena shown in this grouping of potted containers.

appeal; and, forsythia, pansies, flowering kale, hollies, and other evergreens for winter wonders.

Container plants occasionally provide shelter as well. For instance, you can transform part of your yard into a butterfly breeding station by growing host plants such as milkweed or asters in containers. If you want to attract moths, try roses or azaleas. Some birds—sparrows, house finches, and wrens, to name a few—have been known to use hanging baskets as a place to build their nests.

WHAT'S A HOST PLANT?

Host plants serve as incubating stations for butterflies and moths, places where the females can lay eggs. When these winged wonders move on to the next stage of metamorphosis and become larvae or caterpillars, they proceed to eat their way through their former nursery to fuel their prodigious growth, using opposable toothed mandibles that can only be seen with a magnifying glass. As the caterpillar grows, it molts its outer layer of skin from four to six times, much like a snake. Once the caterpillar has eaten its fill, it casts off its final skin and enters the third stage, the pupal phase, where it generally disappears into a case. That case is known as a chrysalis in the case of butterflies and a cocoon if the pupa is a moth. A magnificent winged adult emerges anywhere from one week to several months later, depending on the species.

The chrysalis of the queen butterfly

While adult butterflies and moths generally find a variety of nectar-producing plants appealing, caterpillars typically have very specialized diets. For instance, fodder for the sleepy orange caterpillar consists mostly of senna. Monarch caterpillars feed solely on milkweed, also known as butterfly weed, while cinnabar moth caterpillars eat ragwort. Both these plants not only supply monarch and cinnabar caterpillars with sustenance, but they also increase their survival odds because they are poisonous to many of their predators.

The queen butterfly emerges from its chrysalis. Once fully emerged, the adult will hang upside-down by its legs for several hours until its soft, wrinkled wings fully unfold and harden for flight.

Caterpillars are such picky eaters that butterflies are very particular about where they lay their eggs. And how do female butterflies know which plants to use as hosts for their young? Special taste receptors located in the feet of butterflies both sense sweet liquids and allow many species to "feet taste" the leaves, ascertaining the plant's suitability as a host. Moths have similar taste receptors in their antennae. In addition, both butterflies and moths identify plants by their shapes, colors, and odors. Still, favored host plants for any given species may differ from place to place because taste preferences can vary from one region to the next.

Here the queen butterfly seeks out nectar-rich flowers, such as the lantana.

Clay and plastic pots filled with colorful geraniums and perennials

CONTAINER CHIC

It's not difficult to find all kinds of ready-made pots, planters, and hanging baskets in various styles, colors, materials, and sizes. You'll have a choice of plastic, wood, metal, and glazed pottery or clay containers. In addition, there are moss-lined wire baskets and heavy stone or lightweight faux planters made of polyethylene, polyurethane foam, fiberglass resin, or other materials. The best container for your situation depends on your climate and which plants you intend to put in it.

Made of wicker, wire, plastic, or wire mesh, lightweight pots have the advantage of being portable, allowing you to vary your landscape with the seasons. And using ready-made, lightweight hanging baskets—generally made of plastic or wire-mesh lined with sphagnum moss or a preformed liner—is an easy way to add a vertical dimension to your wildlife habitat. However, because most plastic pots eventually deteriorate in the sun, they aren't the best choice for long-term applications. If what you have in mind

are container plantings that will stay in one place indefinitely, then heavier ceramic, stone, or cast iron pots will work well for you. But keep in mind that without help from a strong friend or access to a sturdy hand dolly, they can be difficult to maneuver—especially when filled with moist soil. Finally, there are clay pots. In addition to their aesthetic appeal, clay and other porous containers offer practical advantages. They tend to be more durable than plastic pots, and their greater breathability prevents the soil from becoming soggy or waterlogged. On the other hand, they dry out faster and therefore need to be watered more often. In fact, during summer's heat, a moisture-loving plant in a small porous clay pot may need watering several times a day.

Size matters when choosing a container, especially when growing shrubs, trees, or multiple plant displays. Be sure your container is large enough to accommodate plants, and allow room for spreading roots. The minimum container for a small planting

or single plant display is 10 inches in diameter. This is one instance where bigger is always better. Larger containers are less subject to temperature fluctuations, and because they hold more soil, plant roots stay moist for longer periods of time.

Whatever pot catches your fancy, be sure it has excellent drainage. If you think a container isn't going to drain properly, you can always add holes to the bottom. An electric drill equipped with a masonry bit works well for drilling stone and ceramic containers. Also, pots will drain better if they're not in direct contact with the ground. Set the container on top of bricks, stone, or an upside-down pot. You can also use pottery feet (sold at nurseries and garden centers) to elevate the container.

Of course, items found at thrift stores, yard sales, or even around the house can function as unique containers. Grow nectar-rich flowers in an outdated red wagon, vintage washbasin, or rusty wheelbarrow. Recycle a discarded wooden tool caddy, old crock, or leaky birdbath into an appealing planter for annuals and perennials that offer a source of seeds for wildlife. Even an unused birdcage, wooden crate, or wicker basket—essentially any container suitable for hanging that has adequate drainage—can serve as an attractive hanging basket. With a little imagination, just about anything (including the kitchen sink) can be a practical yet distinctive container for growing plants.

Even an unused chair can be turned into an attractive planter. Here's one filled with a variety of sedums.

This grouping of container plantings featuring mostly sedums in our front courtyard garden is just one example of how you can position pots containing one type of plant at different heights and mix together different varieties.

A watering can makes a great container for trailing ground covers, dwarf hostas, and other wildlife-friendly plants.

DESIGN TECHNIQUES

Container plantings are certainly a boon to backyard wildlife, but they're also a great way to enhance your home and yard. They make boring entrance areas inviting and exciting, add warmth to interior courtyards, and adorn porches, patios, walls, and doorways with color and texture.

Of course, one of the great things about potted plants, planters, and hanging baskets is that you can move them about. That means you can alter your landscape from season to season. Because containers can be brought indoors to overwinter, you can grow tropical or tender plants that might not otherwise survive if they had to spend the entire year outdoors in a cold climate.

Whether you start out with just a solitary hanging fuchsia or try your hand at a more complex design, let your creativity loose and have fun. A wide range of nectar, seed- and fruit-bearing plants, some of which are listed in chapters 3 and 4, can be grown in containers. You can keep it simple by featuring a single plant. Hanging baskets of various sizes will accommodate anything from plants that are good sources of seeds, such as impatiens, marigolds, or zinnias, to berry-bearing shrubs, such as cotoneaster or miniature roses, all of which will draw a variety of birds. You can also plant Japanese maple, hibiscus, dwarf willow, or red fountain grass in larger containers. And don't forget that you can

A great place to display hanging baskets is near a doorway. The flowering basket shown here is just beginning to bloom with petunias, verbena, and bacopa.

always practice your wildlife zoning skills by setting pots featuring a single plant species at various levels. Use bricks or cement blocks, as well as plant stands, pedestals, wooden stools, or even pots turned upside down to stagger your container plantings.

You can also combine trailing, bushy, and upright plants—either by grouping pots, each containing a single species, or by planting several species in one container. Put together a butterfly buffet featuring chaste tree underplanted with heliotrope and trailing scaevola. Or combine red-flowering penstemons with veronica and trailing geraniums for a small-scale garden hummingbirds will find hard to resist. Create a dramatic display in a hanging basket by combining cascading chrysanthemums, floss flower, trailing verbena, and petunias. Don't be surprised if you spot monarch butterflies and tiger moths sipping nectar from the verbena plants.

When choosing plants for your container garden, remember to think beyond the confines of a pot. This large clay container filled with trailing mint has added appeal for butterflies, hummingbirds, and moths when surrounded by flowering tobacco growing up around the container.

Once you've chosen your plants and put them in containers of various kinds, plan where you're going to put those containers to work. Use potted plants to fill in bare spaces in a newly planted perennial bed or border. Or you can stagger them on steps, encircle a tree, or use them to border a walkway or path. The best location for most hanging baskets is a bright, sheltered area that's out of the way (but within easy reach for watering). Great places to display hanging baskets include patios, porches, decks, and near doorways—but don't stop there. You can hang baskets from a balcony, arbor, gazebo, or even suspend them from trees. It doesn't matter if you plant annuals for an explosion of seasonal color, group perennials for a more permanent effect, or include a combination of the two—hummingbirds, butterflies, and moths will come to visit.

SOIL SAVVY & PLANTING PARTICULARS

An advantage of container gardening is that because you fill the pots and planters with a rich potting soil mix, plants will likely thrive from the start. I often enhance purchased potting mix by using one part rich compost or aged manure (manure allowed to sit undisturbed six months or more) to four parts commercial mix—preferably one with peat moss, forest byproducts or compost, as well as perlite, vermiculite, or pumice to provide added aeration and drainage.

When a container plant dries out completely, it's best to set the container in a pan or large tub of water. This allows the root ball to act as a wick and slowly rehydrate the soil. Large containers too heavy to lift can be watered slowly from above so that the water seeps into the soil.

To plant, first moisten the potting mix and then fill the container a quarter to three-fourths full. The amount of potting mix you initially put in depends on the root space the new plants need. Make sure the top of the root ball sits about 1 to 2 inches below the container's rim. Next, remove plants from their original pots and gently loosen the roots with your fingers. Set plants in their new containers at about the same depth as they were in the original pots. Fill with additional moist potting mix, press the plants firmly in place, and then water thoroughly.

The container's size and the number of plants you've selected, as well as their characteristics, and growth habits, will determine spacing, regardless of whether they're annuals or perennials. A 10-inch container usually accommodates about three to five plants; a 14-inch container will house five to nine plants. Generally, you'll space plants closer together in a container than in a flowerbed or border, and, of course, you can space smaller plants, such as lobelia or alyssum, closer together than you can larger plants. When planting trees, shrubs, and other vertical plants in a container, you can still create a full, lush effect by underplanting with low-growing flowers, ground covers, or plants that cascade or trail. Remember: different plants have different needs. Some perform best in sun, others in shade—so situate them accordingly. And don't forget to make sure plants sharing the same container have compatible moisture and light requirements.

Make your own homemade potting mix by combining equal parts compost, moistened peat moss, and perlite, pumice, or vermiculite. The white specks visible in this mix are perlite. If you're planting moisture-loving plants or using pots that dry out quickly, use vermiculite as the aeration material instead.

MAINTENANCE TIPS

Plants confined in containers often need to be watered and fed more frequently. How often depends on the container's size and type, as well as the time of year and where you've placed the container—in the hot sun or the cool shade.

When it comes to determining the need for water, let your finger be your guide. If the soil feels dry about 1 to 2 inches below the surface, then it's time to water. Most plants prefer soil that's kept slightly moist at all times. Just be sure to water thoroughly until water drains out the bottom.

Container plants need nourishment during the growing season: feed about every two to three weeks with a water-soluble fertilizer or apply a slow-release organic fertilizer two to three times a year. Flowering plants do best with a fertilizer high in phosphorus (such as 5-10-5), while foliage plants thrive on extra nitrogen (like 10-5-5). We often fertilize our container plants with aged pigeon or rabbit manure or with earthworm manure (called earthworm castings, they are available at most garden centers and nurseries).

Occasional pruning will help manage overzealous growth and increase production of berry-producing shrubs. Likewise, pinching back leggy stems or faded flowers encourages plants to produce more blooms over a longer period of time. This is especially important for most nectar-bearing flowers, such as chrysanthemums or pincushion flowers. As the end of the season approaches, let spent blooms remain so they can mature into a seed feast for hungry birds.

Window Box GARDENS

There's a certain charm about window box gardens that sets them apart from other types of container plantings. They heighten a home's beauty by placing a gorgeous display of colorful flowers at a window.

Plants that are appropriate in hanging baskets also generally work well in window box gardens. Yet the options don't end there. Taller and larger specimens that might overpower a hanging basket become dazzling performers in a window box display. Because window boxes are usually viewed from only one side, they're usually planted with taller species in back, low-growing and bushy plants in the foreground, and trailing plants that spill out the sides and front.

Though window boxes are sometimes attached to the inside railing of a patio or porch, they are not as portable as pots or hanging baskets. You can make your displays more interesting—and more attractive to hummingbirds, butterflies, and moths—by changing them with the seasons. You might start with a mix of spring bloomers like sweet peas, candytuft, pansies, sky lupines and trailing periwinkle. Then when summer arrives, replace them with annual phlox, dwarf delphiniums, geraniums, nasturtiums, or petunias.

What's nice about creating a display of annuals is that you can leave them in their original pots and just pop them right in the window box. As each annual ends its performance, take out the pot and replace it with another plant for a continuous display that lasts through the seasons.

WINDOW BOX PLANTS THAT MEASURE UP

BACKGROUND
(large plants and vertical growers)

- **annual lupine** (*Lupinus nanus*)
- **cardinal flower** (*Lobelia cardinalis*)
- **columbine** (*Aquilegia* spp.*)
- **chrysanthemum**
  (*Chrysanthemum* spp.)
- **crocosmia** (*Crocosmia* spp.)
- **delphinium** (*Delphinium* spp.)
- **dwarf sunflower** (*Helianthus* spp.)
- **flowering tobacco** (*Nicotiana* spp.)
- **heliotrope**
  (*Heliotropium arborescens*)
- **hummingbird mint** (*Agastache* spp.)
- **gayfeather** (*Liatris spicata*)
- **gladiolus** (*Gladiolus* spp.)
- **meadowsweet** (*Astilbe* spp.)
- **penstemon** (*Penstemon* spp.)
- **snapdragon** (*Antirrhinum majus*)

FOREGROUND
(low-growing or bushy plants used as fillers)

- **African daisy** (*Osteospermum* spp.)
- **amethyst flower** (*Browallia* spp.)
- **California fuchsia** (*Zauschneria* spp.)
- **candytuft** (*Iberis* spp.)
- **catmint** (*Nepeta* spp.)
- **dianthus** (*Dianthus* spp.)
- **dwarf aster** (*Aster* spp.)
- **dwarf hosta** (*Hosta* spp.)
- **dwarf zinnia** (*Zinnia* spp.)
- **floss flower**
  (*Ageratum houstonianum*)
- **gazania** (*Gazania* spp.)
- **geranium** (*Pelargonium* spp.)
- **impatiens** (*Impatiens walleriana*)
- **marigold** (*Tagetes* spp.)
- **nasturtium** (*Tropaeolum majus*)
- **petunia** (*Petunia* x *hybrida*)
- **salvia** (*Salvia* spp.)
- **sea pink** (*Armeria* spp.)
- **speedwell** (*Veronica* spp.)

TRAILING
(trailing species that spill over the sides and front)

- **caraway thyme**
  (*Thymus herba-barona*)
- **creeping Jenny**
  (*Lysimachia nummularia*)
- **creeping zinnia**
  (*Sanvitalia procumbens*)
- **dwarf periwinkle** (*Vinca minor*)
- **ivy geranium**
  (*Pelargonium peltatum*)
- **nasturtium**
  (*Tropaeolum majus, T. peregrinum*)
- **parrot's beak** (*Lotus berthelotii*)
- **petunia** (*Petunia* spp.)
- **prostrate rosemary**
  (*Rosmarinus officinalis*)
- **rose moss** (*Portulaca grandiflora*)
- **scaevola** (*Scaevola* spp.)
- **sedum** (*Sedum sieboldii*)
- **verbena** (*Verbena* spp.)

* Spp. is the abbreviation for the plural of species.

DID YOU KNOW?

Although most moths are nocturnal, there are some exceptions. For example, you can spot two species of sphinx moths, the hummingbird clearwing and the white-lined sphinx, flying by day.

A white-lined sphinx moth sips nectar from a verbena 'Homestead Purple'.

Planting a Moss-Lined Wire Basket

Here's a lush, versatile hanging basket that's sure to find a home in your garden.

Damp moss is used to line the bottom and sides of this wire basket.

Gently insert the root ball of a plant into the side of the moss-lined basket.

MATERIALS

Wire basket

Sphagnum moss, enough to line the basket

Potting mix

Plants, such as fuchsias, petunias, creeping zinnias, geraniums, sweet alyssum, verbena, ivy, ornamental grasses, scaevola, mints, catmint, sedums, marigolds or morning glory

Compost

Swivel hook or a bracket designed to hold the basket's weight

Chain, wire, rope, or other durable hanger (a pulley hanger allows you to easily raise or lower the basket)

INSTRUCTIONS

1. Line the basket with a thick layer of wet sphagnum moss, and then fill the basket about one-third full with moistened potting mix.

2. Starting a few inches above the base, poke planting holes in the sides of the moss, and then gently insert the root ball of each plant into the basket, working from the outside in. Continue planting in tiers up the sides, filling the basket with the moistened mix as you go to cover the roots after each new level has been planted.

3. Once you've worked your way to the top, add plants to the center of the basket, and then fill the spaces around the edge. Cover the roots with additional mix and top with a layer of compost. Water thoroughly and let the container hang in a shady, protected area for several days to allow the plants to adjust to their new environment before moving to its designated location.

A window box garden filled with butterfly flowers lines a stone window ledge.

Nectar Flower Window Box

This window box is as appealing to you as it is to butterflies, moths, and hummingbirds. The nectar-rich plants featured here include the African daisy, gazania, dwarf asters, chrysanthemums, and trailing verbena.

INSTRUCTIONS

1. Place the aluminum screen or a thin layer of gravel in the bottom to keep the potting mix from washing out. Partially fill the box with a lightweight potting mix.

2. Arrange the nectar-rich plants to your liking, and then plant: keep taller plants in the middle or scattered in back, low-growing and bushy plants in the foreground, and trailing plants along the edges so they can spill out the front and sides.

3. You don't necessarily have to put your window box anywhere near a window. Rest it on a balcony, porch, or deck railing. Or place it on a large rock or on top of stacked brick or stone in your garden.

MATERIALS

Planter

Aluminum screen (5 x 35 inches) or small gravel

Lightweight potting mix*

Assorted nectar-rich plants

*Lightweight potting mix doesn't contain any soil. Instead, it's a mixture of organic and inorganic ingredients. It has the advantage of draining well and tends to be more sterile than mixes containing soil.

Chapter 2

DREAMING BIG

You've taken a few small steps: you've planted a patch of sunflowers, a sheltering tree, and a few berry-producing shrubs, or you've hung several hanging planters filled with nectar-producing flowers here and there. And your efforts have been rewarded. When you look out your window, there's a much better chance you'll be able to watch butterflies flitting about or a junco scratching the ground for seeds. It's made you ambitious. In fact, you've begun to dream of turning most, if not all, of your yard into a wildlife garden.

Almost any project can seem overwhelming unless you have a good plan to help break it down into manageable bits. Think of the planning phase as the organizational tool that takes you from concept to a final design that maximizes your yard's appeal to winged wildlife. This chapter will guide you through the planning process—from analyzing your site and identifying your wildlife needs to organizing your ideas and defining your design. And since you're designing the garden yourself, you won't have to spend a fortune to have the best of both worlds: a wildlife sanctuary and a beautifully landscaped yard the whole family will enjoy.

Assessing Your
PROPERTY

Take a journal and wander through your yard with your eyes wide open, taking notes and drawing simple sketches. Although you can take inventory at practically any time of year, it's probably best to engage in this exercise at some point in the fall or winter so you'll be ready to start planting your wildlife garden in the spring or early summer. You will want to look for your existing landscape's obvious and not-so-obvious features, such as the trees and shrubs in current beds and borders. In addition, record weather patterns, topography, site exposure, and any other factors that might influence your design. Be sure to walk through at different times of the day, or even month, so you're familiar with your property's various microclimates. Note the areas and amounts of sun or shade, the wind conditions and patterns, soil texture and type, low spots (which create potential frost pockets), wet sites, slopes, and grades. And don't forget to jot down which views you want to enhance or block.

Consider your existing landscape and its vegetation from a bird's eye point of view. Those few small steps you've already taken—the patch of sunflowers or the wildlife-friendly trees and shrubs—will serve as the starting point for the more far-reaching landscape design project you now have in mind. Ask yourself whether there are any

American goldfinch in an oak tree

trees or shrubs that offer little in the way of food or shelter? What plants seem to be attracting birds, butterflies or other winged wildlife? Perhaps, for example, you notice local hummingbirds and butterflies flocking to a patch of native flowers while avoiding your hybrid flowerbed. Do you hear birds singing in a particular tree, or do they seem to be taking refuge beneath certain shrubs? Decide which existing trees, shrubs, or significant plantings provide shelter, breeding sites, and a valuable source of food, such as seeds, fruits, nuts, or nectar. You might consider removing plants that don't make the grade or cast too much shade in your yard, especially if a plant looks unhealthy, is unsuitable for the landscape, or is badly situated—if it sits too close to the house, for example.

Birds and butterflies, as well as dragonflies and beneficial insects, benefit from a good mix of open sunny areas and shady sites. Ideally, about half your yard should be in open sun, a fourth in partial sun/shade (four hours or less of bright light on a summer day), and the remaining area in shade—for instance, what you might find underneath the canopy of a broad-leaved tree.

Since a lawn wasn't practical in this space, we created a path and then planted mounds of different thymes between the stones.

ASSETS &
IMPERFECTIONS

Every yard has its good and bad points. Your job is to keep the plantings and hardscapes (or structural elements) that contribute to your overall design and to think about how you can play up the positive features while disguising, modifying, or eliminating any negative ones. Maybe a nectar-rich flowering vine rambling through an evergreen hedge will enhance your view. You can dress up an unattractive fence with fruiting or flowering vines or grow a row of evergreen shrubs that provide wildlife with shelter and screen out unsightly views. Bring life to a boring patio or path by growing mat-forming ground covers to fill in empty spaces between stones and other pavers. Wildlife will appreciate these touches, and you'll enjoy the infusion of Old World charm.

Even poor soil can be modified with a few additions. A thick layer of tightly compacted gravel that filled the area in front of our house didn't discourage Rick and me from putting in the Mediterranean courtyard of our dreams. We bought planting mix in bulk and filled several sweeping stone beds we had already built—most raised to only a foot in height. The plants flourished in the loamy soil and, as a result, so have the birds, butterflies, moths, bees, syrphid flies and other beneficial insects.

Steep slopes, wood patches, rock piles, tree stumps, and boulders are actually positive features when it comes to the wildlife landscape. For example, rocks and boulders located in sunny sites are prime basking spots where butterflies can absorb the surface heat and soak up the sun, plus the stones bring character to the landscape. Cotoneasters, creeping junipers, and other ground covers stop erosion on steep slopes and banks while providing a valuable shelter and foraging site for ground-feeding birds.

A tapestry of lavender, heaths, and heathers turn this slope into a wildlife asset by providing shelter and future food sites for ground-feeding birds and various butterflies.

Tree stumps are a gold mine for wildlife. They can house insects, serve as pedestals for birdseed, and hold shallow pools of water for beneficial insects. You can also use them as planters or surround them with plants that attract wildlife. Coral bells, shown here, entice both hummingbirds and butterflies with nectar.

The Long and Short of PLANNING

Before you take pen and paper in hand to make a wish list, decide on a preliminary budget. Keep in mind that this is a preliminary budget, so you'll need to estimate the costs of materials, including any plants, retaining walls and other hardscapes, irrigation, soil, and accessories—plus any outside labor expenses. If you find yourself overbudget once you've finalized your plan, try changing, altering, or simplifying your ideas before paring down your list. Another option is to landscape in phases, adding as your budget allows (see pages 28 and 33).

Don't forget to let the principles of diversity and wildlife zoning guide your plans as you begin to decide what additions you're going to make to your yard. A good place to start is to include at least one or two large trees, several groupings of smaller trees and shrubs, and no less than one clump of conifers for winter shelter. You'll be guaranteed an attractive garden for months on end if you make sure that you have plants with overlapping blooming cycles.

In addition, trees, shrubs, and vines that provide fruit during different seasons create year-round interest. Mix annuals with showy ornamental grasses with their fabulous, colorful plumes. Add plants with long-lasting foliage, fruit, flowers, or seedheads, and you'll enjoy continuous, captivating color.

Don't forget to include a grouping or two of ornamental grasses, such as the carex and various sedges shown here.

Now consider features that will beautify your space and help meet wildlife needs. What type of water feature would you like to add? How many bird feeders do you envision? What about nesting boxes? Take into account arbors, trellises, or even a gazebo or pergola covered with vines for wildlife to cling to and climb. Complete your wildlife sanctuary with stone or bark pathways, protective hedgerows, and sloped or banked terrain.

This sunflower may have passed its peak bloom, but the seed-filled heads are at just the right stage for this American goldfinch.

A private place where you can retreat and enjoy the view is essential in any garden, whether it's a cozy bench like this one nestled under a clematis-covered arbor, a comfy chair overlooking a bird-feeding station, or an inviting swing sheltered by a tree.

LANDSCAPING IN PHASES

Any significant project comes with costs: money, time, and effort. A well-equipped wildlife garden is no exception. Regardless of how grand your landscape plan is, you can achieve your goal by breaking the process into manageable phases and spreading out the costs.

Before adding to your landscape, first remove any existing plantings or hardscapes that you don't want in the final design. Also be sure to move any plantings or structures you want to relocate.

Feeders entice a variety of birds, including this white-breasted nuthatch.

A typical three-year timeline for a large-scale redesign of your yard might go as follows:

FIRST YEAR: Establish the essentials: trees and shrubs. They are the foundation for any wildlife garden, and they take the longest to reach a significant size. You can wait to plant smaller, faster-growing shrubs in the second year, if necessary.

Next, mark out areas where you will be putting in garden beds, and install appropriate edging material for containing raised beds. Then install any arbors or trellises.

Add accessories, like baths to supply water, bird feeders, and nest boxes, as well as mud puddles and basking stones for butterflies. They're simple to make and install, and you'll be gratified by an immediate increase in your backyard wildlife population.

SECOND YEAR: Plant any remaining small shrubs, and then seed or lay out sod for any additional lawn area. Next, add irrigation where needed (such as in beds and borders) and then plant the garden beds you've established in the first year with perennials, annuals, ground covers, and vines. Keep in mind that these plants have more impact and appeal when planted in groups, called "planting in drifts," or in odd numbers. Now create any paths or walkways.

THIRD YEAR: Fill in the spaces between shrubs and slow-growing perennials with colorful container plantings, fast-growing annual climbers, and additional annuals. Install larger-scale water sources, such as a bog or, if you're really ambitious, a pond, waterfall, or that lion's-head fountain you've had your eye on. And now that more winged creatures have moved into your yard, don't forget you'll need an inviting place from which to enjoy the view—a gazebo, a bench beneath the arbor, or even an outdoor living room.

THE MASTER PLAN

Basic design elements are just as essential to a productive wildlife habitat as they are to creating an aesthetically pleasing garden for people, a place where they'll be more than happy to spend time observing winged creatures. Our courtyard garden is a great example of how good design can benefit both humans and wildlife. Actually, what we wanted to do was re-create the experience of the time we had spent in Monte Carlo and Northern Italy—hence, the Mediterranean garden. While designing a courtyard garden for wildlife wasn't our primary objective, the influx of wildlife was a natural side effect of carefully incorporating design elements into our plan.

These basic design elements include unity, variety, and an accent or focal point. Unity brings a sense of harmony to the garden through a color scheme, a continuing thread of mass plantings, or through the repetition of some plant form or design element. For instance, birds are more apt to flock to a group of sunflowers than to a solitary plant, and wildlife seeking a specific color or type of vegetation is likely to investigate a cluster of plants. Variety offers a selection of plants essential for supporting wildlife diversity, plus it adds visual excitement and brings the garden to life. One important way to add variety is to include plants that provide seasonal beauty—and seasonal sustenance—throughout the year. A focal point catches your eye and invites you in. Garden structures, archways, fountains, ponds, or a prominent bed add emphasis to an

The lion's-head fountain in our courtyard garden serves as the focal point along our walk.

area. More importantly, they provide necessities such as food, shelter, and water for our wildlife friends.

The color, texture, and shapes of plants and other garden elements contribute to your overall design. You can accomplish a great deal with your color choices: for example, you can create different moods, depending on whether you've chosen flowers in warm or cool shades. Texture—whether in the form of foliage, buds or flowers, fruit, bark, or branches—reveals subtle distinctions between light and shade while appealing to your senses of touch and sight. Form, or the shape of a plant, gives a garden structure, substance, depth, and a dynamism that will appeal to a variety of wildlife species. For example, picture a birdbath in the middle of a flowerbed full of small, static plants. Now, picture that same birdbath with swaying ornamental grasses planted underneath.

The walk along our courtyard garden utilizes basic design elements by incorporating a varied selection of plants essential for supporting wildlife diversity. In addition, continuing drifts of color featuring shades of purple, gray, and green bring unity to this space.

A vignette can be as complex as an outdoor living room or as simple as this collection of birdhouses on a backyard wall.

CREATING VISTAS & VIGNETTES

As with any successful design, it's important to let form follow function. Garden vistas and vignettes are good ways to accomplish that goal. A garden vista creates a sense of depth by drawing the eye through an open space to a distant view or prospect while a vignette is an attention-grabbing scene. The process of creating a vignette is much like framing a beautiful view by looking through the lens of a camera.

A garden vista not only draws your eye to a view, it also creates an avenue that functions as a flight path for winged wildlife. A vista, for example, can feature borders of multilevel plantings surrounding a narrow expanse of lawn. Showcase a fountain, birdbath, or even a special butterfly garden at the end for a magnetic focal point that lures you in. You can also create inviting vistas in small spaces by constructing a meandering path that leads to a vine-covered arbor and a comfortable bench. Remember that in general, meandering paths and undulating lines of vegetation look more natural and are far more inviting than rigidly straight and symmetrical lines.

Vignettes can be simple or complex. The scene might include a garden bistro set surrounded by a group of wildlife-friendly potted plants staggered at different heights. How about a butterfly feeding station surrounded by a bed of wispy butterfly-attracting plants like fern-leaf yarrow, cosmos,

and Russian sage? A birdbath placed in the middle of a small, fragrant herb garden tucked off to the side can be especially enticing to all the senses. Whatever vignette you decide on, it's usually best to keep it low, airy, or off to the side. What you don't want to do is place a tall structure or a cluster of shrubs or small trees in an area that blocks your view to the outdoors.

When planning your wildlife garden, be sure to walk and view the prospective area from all vantage points—the street, your front driveway, your neighbor's yard, and even from inside your home. After all, why limit yourself to thinking of the outdoors as the only place to enjoy your garden? Large windows and French doors offer the perfect opportunity to take pleasure in your garden from inside your home.

With a good plan and a little luck, you might even create a chance to view wildlife up close. I actually discovered this quite by accident. When the courtyard garden went in, it greatly improved the view from my office. Placing a vine-covered arbor just six feet from the window enhanced my view even more, especially since the nectar-rich clematis flowers attracted hummingbirds. What I didn't expect was the opportunity to observe a towhee just inches away as it pecked at sunflower seeds sitting in a saucer on the log pile stacked in front of my window. Now that's a room with a view!

Garden vistas are as diverse as the ever-changing landscape. One example is this vine-covered trellis—cloaked in lady banks rose and potato vine—that beautifully frames this wildlife garden while drawing your eye to the oak trees and conifers in the distance.

Julia butterflies basking on stones

...fast tracks

BASKING STONES

Whenever I see butterflies basking, I think back to how good it feels to lie on a warm sunny beach. While soaking up the sun's rays isn't the best thing for humans, it's exactly what these cold-blooded creatures need in order to fly and forage for food during cooler temperatures. You may notice them basking in the sun with outstretched wings, absorbing heat from the sun and from surfaces such as a concrete driveway, wooden deck, dry stream bed, or patch of gravel.

Large rocks and stones are especially valuable since they radiate heat from the sun while providing pockets of moisture formed by rainwater and dew. Place large rocks in a sunny area of your garden that faces south, or create a special niche of basking stones. Mound the rocks over the soil, nestling a few partway into the ground to create a more natural-looking effect. The crevices can then be planted with pockets of sea pink, sweet alyssum, or any low-growing sedum for a nectar source that's always within reach.

DRAW UP A BASE MAP

After measuring the size and shape of your lot and house, draw them to scale on graph paper (see figure 1). Don't be intimidated by the prospect of having to produce a map. When it comes to drawing, my own artistic talent is roughly on a par with that of a first grader, yet even I can do this. You simply decide what unit of measurement each square on the graph paper represents (for example, each square can equal anywhere from one to four square feet) and then draw your house to scale.

You can also generate a base map from a copy of your property survey; your local municipality can supply a copy if you don't already have one in hand. Such surveys usually show property boundaries, lot dimensions, existing buildings (house, garage), and easements. Add physical features, including outbuildings, hardscapes (sidewalks, patios, fences, and arbors, for instance), water sources, power lines, or buried cables, as well as the existing beds or plants that will remain. Note any significant slopes, hills or valleys (represented by angled arrows), sun and wind patterns, and compass directions.

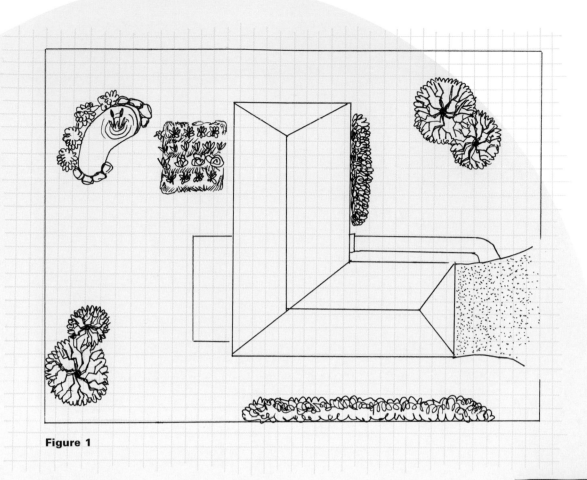

Figure 1

COST-CUTTING MEASURES

Need to shave the costs off the wildlife garden of your dreams? Start by changing, altering, or simplifying your ideas. Perhaps all you need to do is convert your plans for a stone path to a less costly bark-covered path. Modifying a retaining wall by decreasing its overall size or height or converting that elaborate gazebo to a simple, vine-covered arbor with a bench underneath can also help reduce costs.

You can cut costs when buying plants as well. Instead of buying larger shrubs in 5- or 10-gallon containers, opt for the 1-gallon size. And in the case of perennials, smaller plants (in less than a 1-gallon-sized container) cost considerably less and often catch up to their larger cousins in just a couple of years.

How about using your green thumb to start annuals from seed? Or try propagating your own plants for free by dividing overgrown perennials in the fall. Many perennials are good candidates: asters, chrysanthemums, coreopsis, rudbeckia, goldenrod, daylilies, and ornamental grasses, to name a few. Find a vigorous clump (friends or family members are usually happy to share) and carefully dig up the plant to be divided, then use a knife, hand fork, or your hands to separate the plant into smaller clumps. Make sure each new division has two to five vigorous shoots with roots attached, and then cut back the foliage to half its height and replant wherever you'd like.

Turn one plant into several by dividing and replanting perennials in the fall. Rudbeckia is a great candidate. Dividing helps to renew the plant and encourage bigger blooms, plus you'll get free plants in the process.

When soil is less than perfect, raised beds—which you can fill with an enhanced soil mix—are a wonderful way to improve the soil and get plants off to a great start. The raised beds in this newly designed garden are ready for planting.

PUTTING IT ALL TOGETHER

Once you've developed your base map and have all those elements worked out (what plantings to remove, what to add, your wildlife wish list), it's time to bring it all together into a finished design. Create a customized base map of your final design by superimposing on your original base map (see figure 1 on page 33) the planting plan and the elements you've chosen. Indicate placement for trees, beds, and borders, along with arbors, fountains, patios, pathways, or any other hardscapes you wish to include. You can either draw these added elements on an overlay such as tracing paper or make several copies of your base map for sketching in your desired features, hardscapes, and plantings.

Consider computerizing your plan using one of the many landscape design programs that allow you to make changes easily. Garden planning kits are another option. Available at home and garden centers, the kits come complete with a working grid and a variety of stick-on plants in various sizes that work much like the paper doll kits popular in the 1960s. Whichever method you use to draw your final plan, be sure you've incorporated all your essential design and wildlife elements.

 GARDENING BASICS

It's much easier to have a green thumb when you've been blessed with rich loamy soil for most of your gardening life. But if you're like me, you may know all too well how essential good soil is to growing healthy plants because you've experienced the challenge of growing plants in poor soil. That's why it is important to improve the soil, amend the soil, work the soil—however you want to phrase it—so plants will take off and thrive once they're put into the ground.

Start by clearing the planting area of weeds and any existing sod or debris. Then till or dig in a thick layer of organic matter into the top 6 to 8 inches of soil; you can use fertilizers such as compost, dry grass clippings, or aged manure, which is manure allowed to sit undisturbed in a pile for at least six months. (You can safely apply aged manure directly to plants because, unlike fresh manure, it won't burn the vegetation.)

Like wildlife, plants have specific requirements for sun, water, and nutrients—from full sun to shade, almost no moisture to wet feet, slightly poor to rich and fertile soil and, of course, everything in between. Look for the plant label or tag when buying plants; it usually contains important information, such as sun and moisture requirements, growing tips, and the hardiness zone, along with the plant's common and botanical names.

It will help you determine if a plant is suited to your site.

It's best if you buy odd numbers of the same plant and then group them together so they look natural. Once plants are in the ground, mulch the soil with a thin layer of organic matter to conserve moisture and keep weeds down. Water new plantings on a regular basis, provide consistent moisture for annuals, and give young trees a thorough weekly watering during dry months. Even drought-tolerant plants need routine watering the first year or two until they become established.

Chapter 3

The Major players:
TREES & SHRUBS

If you want to attract all kinds of wildlife to your yard, trees and shrubs are great places to start. That's because they are potentially the most valuable and versatile resource in your wildlife garden. Trees and shrubs supply many wildlife essentials—shelter in all four seasons, places to perch, as well as nesting sites and materials. They also function as host plants for butterflies and moths. And then, of course, trees and shrubs provide birds, butterflies, moths, and beneficial insects with edibles in the form of fruit, seeds, nuts, nectar, pollen, insects, and sap. Trees are also important because as the most prominent features in your garden, they provide the landscape with its basic structure. Shrubs make their contribution to landscape design by serving as effective backdrops and foundation plantings (plants placed so they block the view of a building's foundation) and often act as wildlife-friendly hedgerows and screens.

A Japanese maple dressed in brilliant fall foliage

Choosing TREES & SHRUBS

With so many trees and shrubs to choose from, simply making your selections might seem more of a challenge than actually growing them successfully. If you keep the following factors in mind, you'll find that making decisions will be easier.

For starters, be sure the requirements of any shrub or tree under consideration are compatible with your yard's specific soil, water, and light conditions. Once you've narrowed your choices down to trees and shrubs likely to thrive where you intend to plant them, don't limit yourself. You certainly won't want to plant only slow-growing trees that can take up to 50 years to reach maturity—unless, that is, you want to wait decades to see wildlife reap the benefits. Likewise, purchase both evergreens and deciduous trees and shrubs. Both are landscape essentials when it comes to meeting specific wildlife needs.

A Kousa dogwood is the focal point for this shady wildlife garden.

Plants for sale at a farmers' market

After selecting a container-grown coral bark maple, this young gardener is ready to plant.

You can usually find a good selection of trees and shrubs known to do well in your area at your local greenhouse, nursery, garden center, or farmers' market (a great but often overlooked resource). They come as bare-root, balled-and-burlapped, or container plants.

Nurseries dig bare-root plants out of the ground when they are dormant with nearly all the soil removed from the roots. They're generally the least expensive of all the options. Also because they've been dug up during their dormant period, they usually suffer little-to-no stress when transplanted. However, bare-root plants are usually available only in the spring and fall. It's best if you plant bare-root trees and shrubs right away, so you'll need to time your purchases carefully. If you can't put them in the ground immediately, you can mound the exposed roots with moist, loose mulch. Even so, it's best to plant them within a few weeks of bringing them home.

In the case of balled-and burlapped trees and shrubs, nurseries keep the soil around the roots in place by tying burlap or some other material around the root ball. One advantage to balled-

and-burlapped plants is that you cut away the burlap after you've put the plant directly in the ground, so you don't have to struggle with taking it out of the container (something you'll really appreciate if the plant is large). However, if you're working with a large balled-and-burlapped specimen, you might need to call in some extra help when wrestling with a bulky root ball. Balled-and-burlapped plants tend to be more expensive than bare-root plants. They are generally available from late fall to early spring, and as with bare-root plants, they either need to be planted immediately or covered in moist mulch.

Finally, commercial nurseries use containers to grow anything from tiny seedlings to trees measuring 10 feet tall or more. Usually comparable in

cost to balled-and-burlapped varieties, container plants have several advantages. Because more species and varieties are offered in containers and they're available year-round, you'll have a great selection whenever you go to the garden center. And for the most part, healthy container plants establish themselves more quickly. Also, it's possible to buy container trees and shrubs that are smaller, younger, and therefore less expensive than bare-root or balled-and-burlapped plants. The only disadvantage to container plants is that you have to be on the lookout for severely root-bound plants—plants whose tangled roots threaten to break through the pot. Once this happens, it can stunt a plant's growth or girdle the stem, causing death years down the road.

Balled-and-burlapped trees

Example of a root-bound container plant

Example of a good root system
on a bare-root tree

Example of a poor root system on a bare-root tree

Some local nurseries will have a broad selection while others specialize. So save yourself some time and check their ads or their web sites in advance. Remember you also have the option of purchasing trees and shrubs from mail-order catalogs or Internet nurseries, which typically sell dormant bare-root specimens and small potted plants or seedlings. Occasionally, such nurseries offer large container specimens, although the size naturally increases the shipping costs. If you're in search of an unusual plant, a new release, or a specialty variety you can't track down locally, check out the offerings online or in mail-order catalogs.

Buying locally does have the advantage of giving you the chance to examine your potential purchase. When you do, look for a well-developed, symmetrical root system that shows no signs of having dry, damaged, or diseased roots. Of course, it's easiest to actually inspect the roots of a bare-root plant. But if the ties or the root ball appears loose on a balled-and-burlapped plant, it could indicate dried-out roots. When buying large balled-and-burlapped or container specimens, it's particularly important to check for healthy-looking foliage and any signs of disease or pest infestation because you won't be able to see the roots. In the case of container plants in particular, make sure you don't have a root-bound plant. You'll want to avoid buying a plant if you can see roots escaping through drainage holes in the bottom of the container.

PLANTING
TREES & SHRUBS

There are different opinions about the best way to plant trees and shrubs—especially about what size hole is best and what kind of soil to use. I've found the following method works well regardless of whether you're transplanting a bare-root, balled-and-burlapped, or container-grown plant.

DIG A HOLE: Dig a hole 6 to 12 inches deeper and about one-and-a-half to twice the width of the root ball or, in the case of a bare-root plant, the width of the extended roots. Then use your spade to loosen the soil on the hole's sides and bottom and throw in several shovelfuls of loamy soil or compost, mixing it in with the surrounding native soil. Fill the hole with water and allow it to drain.

POSITION THE PLANT: Position the tree or shrub in the hole, and then add enough soil to the bottom so the crown (the part of the plant where the roots and stem meet) is at the correct height. How you do this depends on how the tree or shrub has been packaged.

• **Bare-root plant:** Soak roots in water for an hour or two prior to planting. (I usually add a tablespoon of fish fertilizer for good measure.) Next, spread the roots over a firm, cone-shaped mound in the bottom of the hole; the crown should be 2 inches above ground level.

• **Balled-and-burlapped plant:** Always move a balled-and-burlapped plant by the root ball, not by the stem. Position the plant so the crown is slightly above ground level. Next untie or cut the twine or cage and pull away the burlap by folding it down over the sides of the ball. You can leave the burlap in the hole—it will eventually decompose. However, if the wrapping is plastic or some other nonbiodegradable material,

Digging the hole

Removing the ties on a balled-and-burlapped tree

Carefully sliding a tree out of its container

Gently firming the soil

Filling the basin with water

Mulching around the plant

remove it completely before filling the hole.

- **Container plant:** Take note where the crown is resting in the pot before you start; the top of a container-grown plant's crown should be planted at the same height above the ground as it was in the pot. It's easiest to get the plant out of the container safely if you water it several hours in advance. If the plant doesn't slide out easily, knead the pot by rolling it between your hands a few times or tap the container's bottom and sides. Loosen a tightly matted root system either by scoring the sides of the root system with a knife and gently teasing out a few roots or by loosening the roots with a hand cultivator or fork.

FILL IN THE HOLE: Fill the hole with a mixture of compost and native soil. That way you create a nice transition zone between the usually relatively rich soil of the root ball and the poorer native soil.

FIRM IN THE SOIL: Steady the plant with one hand and then using your other hand or your foot, press down on the dirt. This will stabilize the plant and eliminate any air pockets.

WATER THOROUGHLY: Create a moatlike depression around the plant's base and fill it with water. You might need to fill the depression two or three times until the soil becomes thoroughly saturated. Be sure to allow the water to drain each time before refilling the moat.

SPREAD MULCH AROUND THE PLANT: Spread a 2- to 3-inch layer of mulch around the plant, starting about 6 inches out from the trunk. The mulch helps retain moisture, nourishes the soil, and protects the roots.

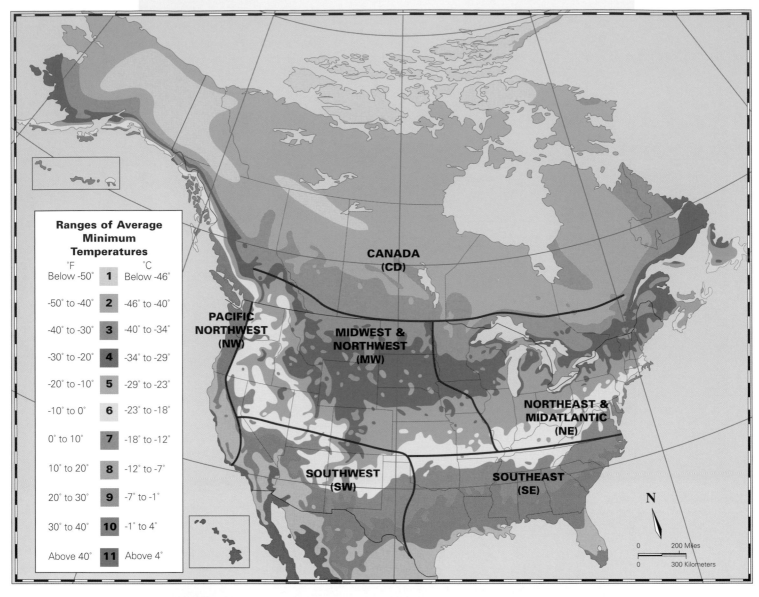

Ranges of Average Minimum Temperatures

°F		°C
Below -50°	**1**	Below -46°
-50° to -40°	**2**	-46° to -40°
-40° to -30°	**3**	-40° to -34°
-30° to -20°	**4**	-34° to -29°
-20° to -10°	**5**	-29° to -23°
-10° to 0°	**6**	-23° to -18°
0° to 10°	**7**	-18° to -12°
10° to 20°	**8**	-12° to -7°
20° to 30°	**9**	-7° to -1°
30° to 40°	**10**	-1° to 4°
Above 40°	**11**	Above 4°

CANADA (CD)

PACIFIC NORTHWEST (NW)

MIDWEST & NORTHWEST (MW)

NORTHEAST & MIDATLANTIC (NE)

SOUTHWEST (SW)

SOUTHEAST (SE)

N

| 0 | 200 Miles |
| 0 | 300 Kilometers |

ZONE & REGION MAP

This map depicts both climactic zones and geographic regions—I've noted both in the following tree and shrub lists. Established by the American Horticultural Society and various U.S. government agencies, including the U.S. Department of Agriculture (USDA), the color-coded climactic zones show the annual average low temperature for a given area, figures based on years of weather data. You'll find the USDA zones listed on most plant tags.

The regions, on the other hand, represent broad geographic divisions of the United States and Canada, areas that have similar soil types and growing conditions. Knowing both your plant hardiness zone and your geographic region will allow you to choose plants likely to survive your winters and flourish in your particular region's growing conditions. Together, these general guidelines will help you put together a winning wildlife garden.

Tree & Shrub LIST

Although this list represents just a sampling of trees and shrubs, no matter where you live in the United States or Canada, you'll be able to find species that can be purchased and grown in your area. A wide range of maturity heights are given since the ultimate height attained depends on growing conditions and the cultivar in question.

The species of birds, butterflies, moths and beneficial insects attracted to these plants will vary, of course, depending on the plant species, where you live, and the surrounding vegetation.

Trees

BIRCH

BIRCH *(Betula* spp.*)*
Zones/Regions: Zones 1 to 10; all regions.

Around 60 species of deciduous trees and shrubs; often grown in clumps of three or more; ornamental bark, colorful fall foliage; attractive male catkins that appear late summer to fall. Grows from 3 to 70 feet in sun to light dappled shade; does best in moderately fertile and moist but well-drained soil.

Varieties: NE, NW, MW, SW, CD: European white birch (*B. pendula*); 15 to 80 feet.
SE, SW, NE, NW: River birch (*B. nigra*); 10 to 50 feet (tolerates dryness and heat).

Wildlife Uses: Flowers (catkins), seeds, insects, nesting sites and material; attracts butterflies, such as adult mourning cloaks which dine on sap; attracts many birds, including pine siskins, redpolls, and chickadees. Caterpillar host plant for butterflies such as swallowtails, mourning cloaks, and admirals, as well as giant silk moths.

CRABAPPLE

CRABAPPLE *(Malus* spp.*)*
Zones/Regions: Zones 2 to 9; all regions.

About 30 species of deciduous trees and shrubs, with most species suitable for a small yard; bears fragrant masses of white, pink, or red flowers in spring; fruits appear in fall and persist into winter; species with the smallest fruits attract the greatest variety of birds. Grows from 6 to 50 feet in full sun to partial shade in slightly fertile, moderate to moist, and well-drained soil.

Varieties: SE: Southern crabapple (*M. angustifolia*), 20 to 30 feet. NE, NW, MW, CD: Siberian crabapple (*M. baccata*); to 40 feet.

Wildlife Uses: Flowers (nectar), flower buds, seeds, fruit, nesting sites, shelter; attracts many birds, including bluebirds, cardinals, waxwings, orioles, finches, and hummingbirds; caterpillar host plant for swallowtail, hairstreak, and viceroy butterflies; comma and question mark butterflies attracted to rotting fruit; flowers also attract bees, including the orchard mason bee.

---

* Spp. is the abbreviation for the plural of *species.*

DOGWOOD

HAWTHORN

HOLLY

DOGWOOD *(Cornus* spp.*)*
Zones/Regions: Zones 2 to 9; all regions.

Around 40 species of mainly deciduous, ornamental trees and shrubs with attractive white, pink, or red flower clusters in spring; colorful foliage in fall; late summer to fall berries that remain through winter. Grows from 6 to 30 feet in full sun to partial shade in well-drained, fertile, and moderately moist soil.

Varieties: NE, SE, NW, MW: Flowering dogwood (*C. florida*); to 30 feet.
NW, NE, MW, CD: Pagoda dogwood (*C. alternifolia*); 10 to 20 feet; best in partial shade.
SW, NW: Pacific dogwood (*C. nuttallii*); to 50 feet.

Wildlife Uses: Fruit, flowers, insects, nesting sites, shelter; attracts birds—such as robins, bluebirds, swallows, and towhees; caterpillar host plant for butterflies species such as whites, blues, and giant silk moths; attracts several species of butterflies, including the spring azure and American snout.

HAWTHORN *(Crataegus* spp.*)*
Zones/Regions: Zones 3 to 10; all regions.

About 200 species of deciduous trees and shrubs; pretty white to pink spring flowers, nice autumn color, and summer through fall fruits resembling tiny apples, often persisting into winter. Grows from 15 to 35 feet tall; likes full sun but will grow in a wide range of soil and moisture conditions.

Varieties: NW, MW, NE, CD: Downy hawthorn (*C. mollis*); to 35 feet.
SE, SW, NW: Lavelle hawthorn (*C. x lavellei*); to 20 feet, semievergreen in warmer climates.

Wildlife Uses: Flowers, fruit, nesting sites, shelter; attracts many birds, including hummingbirds, and several species of butterflies; caterpillar host plant for swallowtail and hairstreak butterflies; flowers appeal to bees.

HOLLY *(Ilex* spp.*)*
Zones/Regions: Zones 4 to 9; all regions.

Over 400 species of trees and shrubs; most are evergreen but some are deciduous; glossy leaves and spring to early summer flowers; yellow, orange, red, or black berries ripening in fall and, in some species, lasting until early spring; both male and female plants needed for berry production. Grows from 3 to 50 feet or more; most prefer full sun; requires partial shade where summers are hot.

Varieties: NW, NE: English holly (*I. aquifolium*); 20 to 60 feet.
SE, SW: Yaupon holly (*I. vomitoria*); 6 to 20 feet.
NE, MW, NW, southern CD: Winterberry (*I. verticillata*); deciduous shrub to 15 feet.

Wildlife Uses: Fruit, shelter (especially in winter), nesting sites; attracts mostly fruit-eating birds, such as bluebirds and robins; host plant for Henry's elfin and holly blue caterpillars; flowers attract spring azure butterflies and bees.

MAPLE

OAK

WILLOW

MAPLE *(Acer* spp.*)*
Zones/Regions: Zones 3 to 9; all regions.

More than 120 species of mostly deciduous, ornamental trees and shrubs with a wide range of attractive leaf shapes, foliage, and autumn color; summer through fall seeds consisting of two small wing-shaped nuts. Grows from 15 to 80 feet in sun to partial shade in fertile, moist, and well-drained soil.

Varieties: SE, SW, NW: Trident maple *(A. buergeranum)*; to 30 feet.
NE, NW, MW: Paperbark maple *(A. griseum)*; to 40 feet.
NW, NE, MW, CD: Silver maple *(A. saccharinum)*; to 80 feet.

Wildlife Uses: Fruit (seeds), buds, insects, summer shelter, nesting sites; attracts birds, including robins, vireos, warblers, finches, wrens, and orioles; provides mourning cloak butterflies with sap; caterpillar host plant for giant silk moths, swallowtail, and mourning cloak butterflies; flowers attract bees.

OAK *(Quercus* spp.*)*
Zones/Regions: Zones 3 to 11; all regions.

Nearly 600 species of deciduous, as well as some evergreen, trees and shrubs; long-lived and stately, some with excellent autumn color; fall fruiting (acorns) persisting into winter; white oak *(Q. alba)*, bur oak *(Q. macrocarpa)*, and red oak *(Q. rubra)* produce abundant acorns. Grows from 15 to 100 feet or more in full sun to partial shade; moisture needs vary by species.

Varieties: NE, MW, NW, CD: Scarlet oak *(Q. coccinea)*; 40 to 60 feet.
NW, SW, SE: Sawtooth oak *(Q. acutissima)*; 40 to 60 feet.

Wildlife Uses: Fruit (acorns), insects, shelter, nesting sites; attracts tree-feeding and nut-eating birds such as jays and woodpeckers; provides adult mourning cloak butterflies with sap; caterpillar host plant for moths such as giant silks and underwings and butterflies such as hairstreaks.

WILLOW *(Salix* spp.*)*
Zones/Regions: Zones 2 to 10; all regions.

More than 300 species of fast-growing, ornamental deciduous trees and shrubs with diverse forms and foliage; flowers (catkins) appearing in late winter to early spring; grows from 3 to 70 feet in full sun (though some species tolerate partial shade); widely adaptable to almost any soil with adequate moisture; most species tolerate poor drainage.

Varieties: NE, MW, NW, CD: Pussy willow *(S. discolor)*; 15 to 25 feet; very attractive catkins.
SW, SE, NE, NW: Weeping willow *(S. babylonica)*; to 40 feet.

Wildlife Uses: Flowers (catkins), buds, seeds, insects, nesting sites; attracts grosbeaks, redpolls, hummingbirds, and others; early nectar source for tortoiseshell, comma, peacock, and spring azure butterflies; caterpillar host plant for mourning cloak, viceroy, blue, and swallowtail butterflies as well as sphinx and underwing moths; flowers also attract many beneficial insects, including nonstinging bees.

CONIFERS

JUNIPER

JUNIPER *(Juniperus* spp.*)*
Zones/Regions: Zones 3 to 9; all regions.

About 60 species of evergreen shrubs and trees, with cones appearing in early fall and persisting into winter; cones develop into fleshy, berrylike fruits; forms vary from spreading horizontal shrubs to upright columnars, some narrow, some broad. Most grow from 2 to 20 feet in full sun to partial shade; tolerates a wide range of conditions and soils but generally best if kept slightly on the dry side.

Varieties: NW, NE, MW, SW, SE: Chinese juniper *(J. chinensis)*; numerous cultivars from spreading shrubs to conical trees.
NE, NW, MW, SW, CD: Common juniper *(J. communis)*; numerous cultivars from upright shrubs to small trees.

Wildlife Uses: Fruit, winter shelter, nesting sites; attracts birds, such as bluebirds, robins, waxwings, brown thrashers, and grosbeaks.

PINE

PINE *(Pinus* spp.*)*
Zones/Regions: Zones 2 to 12; all regions.

Around 110 species of evergreen, coniferous trees and some shrubs with needlelike leaves and attractive seed cones appearing in early fall. Grows from 10 to 100 feet or more in a wide range of climates and conditions, with most preferring full sun and little moisture.

Varieties: NE, MW, NW, CD: Jack pine *(P. banksiana)*; to 60 feet.
NW, NE, SW, MW: Japanese white pine *(P. parviflora)*; to 80 feet. SE, NE, NW: Virginia pine *(P. virginiana)*; to 50 feet.

Wildlife Uses: Seeds, cones, insects, winter cover; attracts birds, including chickadees, grosbeaks, finches, sparrows, jays, and mourning doves; caterpillar host plant for pine white and pine elfin butterflies; provides winter home for monarch butterflies.

SPRUCE

SPRUCE *(Picea* spp.*)*
Zones/Regions: Zones 1 to 10; NE, MW, NW, CD.

Around 40 species of evergreen, coniferous trees and shrubs with stiff, needlelike leaves and attractive, colorful and pendulous cones that appear in early fall. Grows from 6 to 100 feet or more in full sun to light shade with little to moderate moisture; grows best where summers are mild and cool.

Varieties: NE, MW, NW, CD: White spruce *(P. glauca)*; 6 to 80 feet.
NE, MW, NW, CD: Colorado blue spruce *(P. pungens)*; 15 to 100 feet.

Wildlife Uses: Seeds, cones, winter shelter, nesting sites; attracts birds, particularly grosbeaks, chickadees, and nuthatches.

...fast tracks

Weigela

SHELTER PLANTS FOR QUICK COVER

If you need to create shelter and fill in a bare area fast, plants that provide quick cover can be a gold mine for wildlife and humans alike. Many shelter plants are fast-growers that reach for the sky long before slower-growing oaks and dwarf conifers even begin to take off.

Good choices for shelter trees that provide quick cover include most locust, ash, and elm along with eucalyptus, poplar, European white birch, quaking aspen, and (unless you live in the South where it's an invasive species) paulownia. Speedy shelter shrubs include cherry, laurel, Leyland cypress, privet, cotoneaster, and barberry, along with lavatera, spirea, weigela, and, of course, butterfly bush. And don't forget to include a few fast-growing vines, such as honeysuckle, clematis, Virginia creeper, or morning glory.

As an added bonus, trees and shrubs that grow quickly tend to be less expensive than their slower-growing counterparts. That's because nurseries invest less in the way of time or expense before they offer them for sale. And since these plants grow so rapidly, you can purchase one- to two-year-old seedlings or plants. These young plants, which are anywhere from one to three feet in height, will shoot up in no time at all.

BUTTERFLY BUSH

COTONEASTER

ELDERBERRY

BUTTERFLY BUSH *(Buddleja* spp.*)*
Zones/Regions: Zones 4 to 10; all regions except colder parts of the MW and CD.

Around 100 species of deciduous, semi-deciduous, and evergreen shrubs and trees with butterfly-attracting flowers that come in a wide range of colors and hues—even yellow; depending on species, fragrant flowers bloom mostly in summer; some species bloom in spring and summer or in fall and winter. Grows from 5 to 25 feet in full sun or light shade, average soil, and regular water; many species somewhat drought-tolerant once established.

Varieties: All regions, except colder parts of MW and CD: Butterfly bush *(B. davidii)*; 7 to 17 feet.
SW, SE, NW: Orange butterfly bush *(B. globosa)*; fragrant, orange, ball-like flowers; 10 to 15 feet.

Wildlife Uses: Flowers (nectar), seeds, insects, shelter; attracts hummingbirds and some seed-eating birds; flowers attract small insects and a wide range of butterflies, including swallowtails, monarchs, sulphurs, buckeyes, painted ladies, fritillaries, and commas, as well as moths, including the hummingbird clearwing.

COTONEASTER *(Cotoneaster* spp.*)*
Zones/Regions: Zones 3 to 11; all regions.

About 200 species of evergreen, semi-evergreen (keep their leaves for part of the winter), or deciduous shrubs and trees with small white to deep pink flowers that bloom from spring to summer; yellow, black, pink, or, more typically, orange or red berries appearing in fall; some species hold berries into winter. Grows from 1 to 30 feet in full sun (evergreen and semievergreen) to partial shade (deciduous species) in moderately fertile, well-drained soil with little to moderate moisture.

Varieties: SE, SW, NW: No common name, though listed in older references as parney cotoneaster or milkflower *(C. lacteus)*; graceful, arching evergreen shrub; to 8 feet or taller.
NE, MW, NW, CD: Cranberry cotoneaster *(C. apiculatus)*; dense, deciduous shrub; to 3 feet.

Wildlife Uses: Fruit, shelter (some with winter cover), nesting sites; attracts birds, such as waxwings, finches, robins, and towhees; flowers attract hummingbirds, spring azure butterflies, and bees.

ELDERBERRY *(Sambucus* spp.*)*
Zones/Regions: Zones 3 to 10; all regions.

Around 20 species of usually ornamental deciduous shrubs and trees with attractive leaves, flowers, and late summer to autumn berries remaining through winter; shrubs forming dense thickets. Grows from 5 to 25 feet in full sun to light shade in moderately fertile, fairly moist soil.

Varieties: All regions: American elderberry *(S. canadensis)*; 8 to 12 feet.

Wildlife Uses: Fruit, insects, flowers (nectar), shelter, nesting sites; attracts a wide range of bird species, including jays, bluebirds, cardinals, grosbeaks, and nuthatches; flowers attract hummingbirds, swallowtail and hairstreak butterflies, and various beneficial insects.

FIRETHORN

HONEYSUCKLE

ROSE

FIRETHORN *(Pyracantha coccinea)*
Zones/Regions: Zones 5 to 10;
SW, SE, NW, (warmer parts) NE

Less than 10 species of fast-growing evergreen shrubs (semievergreen in colder climates) with masses of brilliantly colored berries of red, orange, or yellow that appear in late summer and fall and persist into winter. Grows from 10 to 15 feet and performs best in full sun to partial shade in rich, well-drained, and moderately moist soil.

Varieties: SE, SW: Narrow-leafed firethorn *(P. angustifolia)*; bushy shrub; to 12 feet high.
NW, NE, SW, SE, warmer parts of CD: Scarlet firethorn *(P. coccinea)*; dense shrub; to 15 feet high.

Wildlife Uses: Fruit, insects, shelter, nesting sites; berries attract fruit-eating birds, including mockingbirds, robins, and cedar waxwings; flowers attract several beneficial insects, including bees.

HONEYSUCKLE *(Lonicera* spp.*)*
Zones/Regions: Zones 2 to 11; all regions.

About 180 species of evergreen and deciduous shrubs as well as climbers and ground covers; valued for their attractive and often fragrant flowers, with summer through early winter berries that are especially appealing to birds; shrubs from 3 to 12 feet; adaptable to most conditions but grows best in full sun to partial shade and in rich, well-drained, and moderately moist soil.

Varieties: SE, SW, NW: Box honeysuckle *(L. nitida)*; dense, bushy evergreen shrub; 6 to 12 feet.
NE, MW, NW, CD: Amur honeysuckle *(L. maackii)*, deciduous purple-stemmed shrub with fragrant white flowers; to 15 feet.

Wildlife Uses: Fruit, nectar, insects, shelter, sometimes nesting sites; attracts birds, including robins, thrashers, orioles, wrentits, and hummingbirds; attracts butterflies, including skippers and swallowtails; caterpillar host plant for admiral butterflies and sphinx moths; flowers attract beneficial insects, including bees and syrphid flies.

ROSE *(Rosa* spp.*)*
Zones/Regions: Zones 2 to 11; all regions.

Around 150 species of mostly deciduous and various evergreen shrubs and vines, with summer and fall fruit (hips) persisting into winter; ranging in height from low-growing ground covers or dense shrubs to arching branches reaching up to 30 feet; generally tolerates a wide range of conditions, though most perform best in full sun and moderately fertile and moist but well-drained soil.

Varieties: The following species are especially attractive to birds:
All regions: Ramanas rose *(R. rugosa)*; vigorous shrub with large, round red hips, to 8 feet.
All regions: Redleaf rose *(R. glauca)*; arching shrub with dark purplish red stems when young, bluish gray leaves, and oblong hips; very striking; to 6 feet tall.

Wildlife Uses: Fruit (hips), insects, shelter, nesting sites; attracts birds, particularly bluebirds, juncos, and grosbeaks; flowers attract Baltimore checkerspot butterflies and bees; caterpillar host plant for mourning cloak butterflies.

SPIREA

VIBURNUM

A chickadee perches on a stem in a white oak tree.

SPIREA *(Spiraea spp.)*
Zones/Regions: Zones 3 to 11; all regions.

Over 70 species of mainly deciduous flowering shrubs with ornamental foliage; spring to fall flowers that come in two distinct forms: the bridal wreath type with arching branches and clusters of white flowers and the shrubby type with white, pink, or red blooms. Grows from 3 to 10 feet in full sun to light shade in fertile, moderate to moist soil.

Varieties: All regions: Japanese spirea *(S. japonica)*; upright and shrubby; to 6 feet.
SE, SW, NE, NW: Bridal wreath spirea *(S. prunifolia)*; graceful arching branches; to 7 feet.

Wildlife Uses: Flowers (nectar), insects, nesting sites, shelter; attracts birds and butterflies, particularly the red-spotted purple butterfly; attracts moths, including checkerspot and tiger moths; caterpillar host plant for spring azure butterflies; flowers attract lady beetles and other beneficial insects.

VIBURNUM *(Viburnum spp.)*
Zones/Regions: Zones 2 to 10; all regions.

Over 100 species of deciduous and evergreen shrubs and trees with diverse foliage, flowers, and forms; summer and fall fruit sometimes persisting into winter. Grows from 5 to 20 feet tall; growing needs vary by species, but most prefer full sun to partial shade in moderately rich and moist but well-drained soil.

Varieties: NE, MW, NW, CD: European cranberry bush *(V. opulus)*; deciduous shrub with arching branches and maple-like leaves; cultivars ranging from 2 to 15 feet.
SE, NE, NW, SW: Doublefile viburnum *(V. plicatum var. tomentosum)*; outstanding spreading shrub with tiered branches and flat umbels of creamy flowers in spring; 8 to 15 feet.
NE, MW, NW, CD: Black haw *(V. prunifolium)*; spreading deciduous shrub with roundish oval leaves; to 20 feet.

Wildlife Uses: Flowers (nectar), fruit (berries), insects, shelter, nesting sites; attracts a variety of birds, including woodpeckers, mockingbirds, finches, bluebirds, robins, grosbeaks; caterpillar host plant for the spring azure butterfly, as well as the sphinx and hummingbird moths; flowers attract red-spotted purple butterflies, some moths, and beneficial insects, including bees.

DID YOU KNOW?

Chickadees prepare a winter food supply by gathering seeds in autumn and storing them in hundreds of hiding places in trees and on the ground. That's a lot of hiding places for a bird to remember, especially for one so small it can fit inside the palm of your hand. Yet as the chickadee gathers seeds in fall, its hippocampus—the area of the brain that deals with organization and memory—expands in volume by about 30 percent in order to accommodate new nerve cells. Once spring arrives, the chickadee brain shrinks back to its normal size.

Chapter 4

The Supporting Cast

Pretty in pink, the flowers of scented geranium tempt a rufous hummingbird.

Now that you've devised your landscape design and selected the trees and shrubs that will serve as the framework for your new wildlife-friendly garden, it's time to turn your attention to flowers, grasses, ground covers, and vines—less conspicuous plants, perhaps, but still vital additions to your garden.

The lists of selected perennial and annual plants included here are just a sampling of the many possibilities at your disposal. However, the lists that follow will give you a choice of plenty of readily available plants that grow in a wide range of regions. Each of these plants, which will appeal both to beginning gardeners and seasoned pros, provides for a variety of wildlife needs.

If you put the principle of diversity into practice and carefully include a mix of perennials and annuals that span the seasons, you'll attract a variety of winged wildlife. At the end of the chapter, you'll find even more inspiration in the form of two garden plans. Since they show you plant-by-plant how to create a night-blooming moth garden and a songbird garden, you can re-create these gardens in your own backyard or mine them for ideas and then put it all together your own way.

(Above) A tiger swallowtail rests on a purple coneflower. Coneflowers are always first-rate in any wildlife garden, attracting birds with seeds and appealing to beneficial insects and butterflies with nectar.

(Upper left) The Ranchman's tiger moth, seen here on a bellflower, often seeks out nectar-rich flowers by day.

Filled with wildlife-friendly trees, shrubs, and a wide selection of perennials, this garden provides for essential wildlife needs.

All-Purpose PERENNIALS

When you need a plant you can depend on, take a look at perennials. These plants offer a broad range of options that will help you both attract wildlife and create an attractive garden, all at the same time.

For starters, because perennials grow for two or more years, these garden mainstays are often a wonderful source of colorful blooms year after year. While most perennials die to the ground after each growing season, emerging almost miraculously from their roots each spring, others keep their leaves throughout the year. And then there are those perennials such as coneflower, coreopsis, penstemon, and sedum that offer the added advantage of being drought-tolerant once they're established, so they can be counted on as a wildlife food source even in years when rain is scarce. If you live in an area that receives at least some rainfall, water-thrifty perennials may well survive an entire growing season without your having to supplement whatever water nature decides to dispense.

The main value of perennials to winged wildlife is as a food source. An assortment of perennials entices birds such as finches, sparrows, and chickadees because they're a good source of the seeds they love. These plants also occasionally serve up the tasty insects so appealing to birds like wrens, nuthatches, warblers, and swallows, as well as to carnivorous winged insects like dragonflies. The flowers of perennials offer sweet nectar to hummingbirds, butterflies, moths, and beneficial bugs such as lacewings and lady beetles. Finally, perennials can supply both shelter and food when they serve as host plants for various butterflies. So browse this list and consider adding at least a few of these ever-useful perennials to your wildlife garden.

Perennials*

ASTERS

ASTERS *(Aster* spp.** *)*
Zones/Regions: Zones 2 to 9; all regions.

Profusion of daisylike flowers in white and varying shades of blue, red, pink, or purple, with most species flowering in late summer and autumn. Grows in full sun from 6-inch compact mounds to tall, spreading plants measuring up to 6 feet in height.

Wildlife Uses: Flowers (nectar), seeds; attracts many birds, including cardinals, goldfinches, chickadees, nuthatches, and towhees; nectar-rich flowers appeal to beneficial insects as well as butterflies like whites, blues, monarchs, skippers, and painted ladies; caterpillar host plant for crescents and painted ladies.

* See page 42 for map showing zones and regions.
**Spp.* is the abbreviation for the plural of *species*.

CHRYSANTHEMUMS

CHRYSANTHEMUMS
(Chrysanthemum spp.*)*
Zones/Regions: Zones 4 to 10; all regions.

Perennials and annuals with showy flowers in a wide range of flower types—from big pompom shapes and spiderlike, tubular florets to single and semi-double forms resembling cosmos, zinnias, or tiny buttons of daisy-like blooms; flowers generally occur summer to fall. Grows 1 to 5 feet in full sun and fairly rich soil.

Wildlife Uses: Flowers (nectar), seeds; attracts many birds, including hummingbirds, along with beneficial insects and butterflies such as sulphurs and monarchs; caterpillar host plant for checkerspots and painted ladies.

CONEFLOWER

CONEFLOWER *(Echinacea* spp.*)*
Zones/Regions: Zones 3 to 10; all regions.

Native to the United States, the genus comprises nine species of perennials, ranging in color from shades of pink to lavender and rose as well as yellow and white; daisylike flowers appearing in summer, followed by late autumn seedheads. Drought-tolerant; grows from 1 to 4 feet in full sun to light shade.

Wildlife Uses: Flowers (nectar), seeds; attracts many birds, including finches, chickadees, nuthatches, and towhees; nectar-rich flowers appeal to beneficial insects, hummingbirds, and butterflies such as skippers, swallowtails, monarchs, and viceroy.

COREOPSIS

COREOPSIS *(Coreopsis* spp.*)*
Zones/Regions: Zones 3 to 11; all regions.

Member of the daisy family, with approximately 80 species of perennials and annuals in shades of yellow, pink, red, and orange, with some bicolored blooms; compact plants with self-seeding tendencies; flowers freely from summer through fall. Drought-tolerant; grows from 2 to 4 feet in full sun and somewhat fertile, well-drained soil.

Wildlife Uses: Flowers (nectar), seeds; attracts birds, including finches, chickadees, sparrows, and other seed-eaters; nectar-rich flowers appeal to beneficial insects and butterflies such as skippers, buckeyes, painted ladies, and pearl crescents.

GOLDENROD

GOLDENROD *(Solidago spp.)*
Zones/Regions: Zones 3 to 10; all regions.

Nearly 100 perennial species; branching clusters of elongated flowerheads bearing tiny golden yellow blooms from mid-summer into fall. Somewhat drought-tolerant; grows easily from 2 to 6 feet in full sun to light shade; will tolerate poor soil.

Wildlife Uses: Flowers (nectar), seeds; attracts many birds, beneficial insects, and butterflies, including hairstreaks, sulphurs, blues, and monarchs; caterpillar host plant for checkerspots.

The caterpillar of the cinnabar moth feeds on plants in the Senecio family, with a particular fondness for tansy ragwort as its host plant. The black and orange rings make this caterpillar easy to recognize.

DID YOU KNOW?

Caterpillars are truly champion eaters. A monarch butterfly larva, for example, gains approximately 2,000 times its weight in two weeks or less. As a result, the foliage of host plants often looks somewhat ragged and defoliated. You may not notice the nibbles if you mingle them among other plantings, confine them to the back of the border, or carve out a corner space of your yard.

MILKWEED

MILKWEED *(Asclepias incarnata; A. speciosa; A. tuberosa)*
Zones/Regions: Zones 2 to 10; all regions.

Upright, woody-based perennials, typically with summer flowers, emerging in clusters of pink, purple, yellow, orange, and bright red; attractive inflated seedpods with silky seeds. Grows from 2 to 4 feet in full sun, with best flower production occurring in fairly rich and moist soil.

Wildlife Uses: Flowers (nectar), seeds; attracts birds and hummingbirds; especially favored by many butterflies, including monarchs, skippers, swallowtails, blues, fritillaries, and hairstreaks; caterpillar host plant for monarch and queen butterflies as well as the milkweed tiger moth.

PENSTEMON

PENSTEMON *(Penstemon spp.)*
Zones/Regions: Zones 3 to 10; all regions.

Resembles its foxglove relative with clumps of tubular to bell-shaped summer flowers. Genus has nearly 250 species, with blooms usually in shades of red or blue but also in soft hues such as pink, peach, purple, salmon, rose, and white; flowers appear on upright terminal spikes, growing from 1 to 5 feet in full sun to light shade; drought-tolerant.

Wildlife Uses: Flowers (nectar), seeds; attracts many birds, including hummingbirds, as well as bees, moths, and butterflies such as skippers and swallowtails. Caterpillar host plant for checkerspots.

SALVIA

Salvia *(Salvia* spp.*)*
Zones/Regions: Zones 4 to 11; all regions.

Nearly 900 species in the genus, with fragrant flowers and colors ranging from pink, salmon, scarlet, and red to shades of purple, blue, and lavender as well as white and yellow; flowers usually appear in summer. Grows from 1 to 5 feet in full sun and well-drained soil.

Wildlife Uses: Flowers (nectar); attracts beneficial insects, hummingbirds, moths and butterflies; caterpillar host plant for painted ladies and hairstreaks.

Lady beetles being released in the garden

DID YOU KNOW?

During the autumn and winter months, adult lady beetles hibernate in clusters ranging from just a few to several hundred. These beneficial bugs seek protection under leaves, rocks, and fallen trees, often assembling in the same spots year after year. Dealers of lady beetles have found colonies in the mountains of California that contained as many as 500 gallons of beetles—and in case you're wondering, there are from 72,000 to 80,000 beetles per gallon.

SEDUM

SEDUM (*Sedum* spp.*)*
Zones/Regions: Zones 4 to 11; all regions.

Diverse group of succulents in a wide range of shapes, sizes, and colors— some are quite hardy in cold climates while others stand up to extreme heat; spring to autumn flowers followed by late autumn and winter seedheads; some form compact mats while others grow to 3 feet tall when flowering. Drought-tolerant; grows in full sun to part shade.

Wildlife Uses: Flowers (nectar), seeds; attracts finches, chickadees, and many other seed-eating birds, as well as hummingbirds; also attracts a variety of beneficial insects and butterflies, including red admirals, commas, and painted ladies.

VERBENA

VERBENA (*Verbena* spp.*)*
Zones/Regions: Zones 3 to 11; all regions.

Diverse group of perennials ranging from sprawling ground covers with rounded flower clusters to erect flowering stalks; blooms late spring to fall in shades of lavender, purple, pink, red, and white. Varying species that grow from 8 inches to 5 feet in full sun to light shade and in well-drained soil; water needs vary by species, with many being drought-tolerant.

Wildlife Uses: Flowers (nectar), seeds; attracts birds, including hummingbirds, as well as sphinx moths and butterflies, such as skippers, swallowtails, and viceroys; caterpillar host plant for blues.

All-Purpose ANNUALS

With a longer blooming period than that of most perennials and shrubs, colorful annuals liven up the interludes between the flowering periods of your prized perennials. Because annuals sprout and die within the space of a single season, their goal is to grow fast and bloom long. That means that each season, annuals offer a plentiful and long-lasting food source for wildlife.

Like perennials, the main value of annuals to wildlife is as a food source. Many annuals offer seeds for a variety of birds and nectar for humming-birds, butterflies, moths, and beneficial insects. Butterflies such as sulphurs and painted ladies use specific annuals as host plants for their caterpillars.

While you can plant some annuals right after the last spring frost has passed, you can plant others as late as halfway through the growing season, and they will still have plenty of time to put on a show. Particularly valuable are the annuals that self-seed. These are plants that die at the end of one season, yet drop seeds that grow the following season, making them function much like perennials. Just be sure to leave the seedheads alone in the fall so they can drop some seeds into the ground.

All of these annuals can be grown in all regions; climactic zones are usually not given for annuals.

BACHELOR'S BUTTONS

BACHELOR'S BUTTONS
(Centaurea cyanus)
Daisy family member from the Mediterranean region and western Asia; flowers late spring to midsummer, usually in shades of blue, with garden forms including pink, red, or white. Erect annual growing from 1 to 3 feet tall in full sun.

Wildlife Uses: Flowers (nectar), seeds; attracts butterflies, beneficial insects, and many birds, including finches, buntings, and sparrows.

CLEOME

CLEOME *(Cleome hasslerana)*
Marginally frost-hardy annual that bears clusters of spiderlike summer flowers until the first frost, in white or shades of pink to purple, followed by slender seed capsules; flowers may self-seed; stems often spiny. Grows from 4 to 6 feet tall in full sun and fertile soil.

Wildlife Uses: Flowers (nectar), seeds, shelter; attracts butterflies, hummingbirds, beneficial bees, and many songbirds.

COSMOS

COSMOS *(Cosmos bipinnatus)*
Showy, daisylike flowers with feathery foliage blooms from summer to fall; flowers appear in a spectrum of colors and forms. Grows from 2 to 6 feet in full sun and average, well-drained soil.

Wildlife Uses: Flowers (nectar), seeds, shelter; attracts hummingbirds, beneficial insects, butterflies—including painted ladies, monarch, buckeyes—and many birds, such as juncos, finches, sparrows, and buntings.

FLOWERING TOBACCO

FLOWERING TOBACCO
(Nicotiana spp.*)
Tubular to bell-shaped flowers in soft shades of green, yellow, pink, red, or white, with fragrant species being most potent at dusk and at night; large leaves often sticky to the touch and covered in fine hairs; many species readily self-seed. Grows from 2 to 8 feet tall in full sun or partial shade.

Wildlife Uses: Flowers (nectar), shelter; attracts birds, butterflies, hummingbirds, and moths.

MARIGOLDS

MARIGOLDS *(Tagetes spp.)*
More than 50 species of fast-growing annuals in red, orange, yellow, mahogany, white, and bicolored varieties, appearing from summer to frost; fernlike, often fragrant leaves. Grows from 6 inches to 4 feet tall in full sun and fertile, well-drained soil.

Wildlife Uses: Flowers (nectar), seeds; attracts birds, including finches and sparrows; nectar rich flowers appeal to butterflies, including sulphurs, buckeyes, and checkerspots and to many beneficial insects; caterpillar host plant for sulphurs.

---

*Spp. is the abbreviation for the plural of *species.*

SUNFLOWERS

SUNFLOWERS *(Helianthus annuus)*
Upright annual with hairy stalks of daisylike flowers that bloom in vibrant yellows, reds, oranges, and browns; fast growing; height ranging from compact 12-inch dwarfs to 12-foot giants. Best grown in full sun and well-drained soil.

Wildlife Uses: Flowers (nectar), seeds; attracts butterflies, beneficial insects, and many birds, including finches, cardinals, chickadees, nuthatches, and juncos; caterpillar host plant for painted ladies and checkerspots.

ZINNIAS

ZINNIAS *(Zinnia* spp.*)*
Central and South American native and longtime garden- and bird-favorite; grows in a diversity of shapes and sizes; typical colors include white, yellow, orange, red, purple, and lilac; heat-loving plants flower in full sun from summer until frost. Grows from 8 inches to 4 feet in fertile, well-drained soil.

Wildlife Uses: Flowers (nectar), seeds; attracts many birds, including finches, chickadees, titmice, and sparrows; nectar-rich flowers appeal to hummingbirds, beneficial insects, and butterflies, especially painted ladies, monarchs, skippers, and swallowtails.

...*fast tracks*

DUST BATHS

Some birds bathe in dust much the same way as they bathe in water. Instead of splashing water over their backs, they nestle down in a soft pile of dust, then shake and flutter their wings while immersing their feathers. Experts believe that dust bathing helps birds rid their feathers of lice, mites, and other parasites.

Allowing a small area of soil to remain bare makes an adequate dust bath. Better yet, create a first-class bath by filling an unused broiler pan or cracked birdbath basin with fine dust, sand and soil, or an equal mix of sand, soil, and sifted ash. Choose a sunny location to place your bath, preferably within easy access of a feeder. You can also construct an "in-ground" dust bath by digging an area 2 to 3 feet square and about 3 to 6 inches deep. Use bricks, stones, or wood to line the edges and define the space. After that, it's simply a matter of sitting back and enjoying the entertainment as you watch the dust fly.

GARDENING BASICS

You'll have no trouble finding places to purchase perennials. They're sold at garden centers, nurseries, farmers' markets, and sometimes even at supermarkets and yard sales. And don't forget to check out mail-order catalogs and the web. Although you'll come across perennials that are packaged, you'll usually buy them as plants in containers—in 4-inch containers as well as one- or two-gallon pots. When choosing a perennial, follow the same guidelines as those for selecting trees and shrubs: make sure the plant's soil, light, and moisture requirements are compatible with those found in your yard and then check the foliage and root system.

Most perennials can be planted from spring to fall. For best results, put the plant in the ground on a cool or cloudy day. If that's not possible, plant early in the morning or evening. Planting in the heat of midday can cause the plant to wilt. Make sure the transplanted perennial is at the same depth as it was in its container. If you want to wait until the weather is more conducive to planting, feel free to keep a perennial in its container for several weeks. Just take care to keep it watered.

If you're in search of annual plants, you can often purchase annual starts at supermarkets as well as at nurseries, garden centers, and farmers' markets. Most are available in seedling containers composed of individual cells known as six-packs. You can also buy slightly larger plants in 4-inch pots or, as the season progresses, even larger plants in gallon containers.

Blanket flowers with a tree borer

The most economical way to fill in those empty garden spaces is to grow annuals from seed. And the simplest way to grow annuals is to sow the seeds directly in your garden. The best time to do this is usually just before or right after your last spring frost has passed. The crucial step when sowing any seeds is to provide a smooth bed, so the seed can sprout unimpeded by weeds, rocks, or soil clumps. After clearing the bed of any debris and breaking down clods or clumps, cover the area to be planted with a 2- to 3-inch layer of compost or other decomposed organic matter. Mix, dig, or till the organic matter to a depth of 6 to 8 inches, and then smooth the surface with the back of a tined rake.

Many flower seeds appear as tiny specks that can get lost in the shuffle, and you can accidentally plant them in masses. If plants are grown too closely together, they'll be weak, spindly, and more prone to pests and disease. Also, overplanting means thinning later, and who wants to do that? A little sand or vermiculite mixed in with the seeds beforehand will help remedy the situation. Cover seeds according to the growing instructions listed on the packet, and keep the seed bed moist until sprouts appear; that might necessitate watering the bed daily. Extremely tiny seeds sprout more easily if they're covered with a thin layer of vermiculite or finely sifted compost .

A praying mantis sits motionless, waiting to strike.

NATURAL PEST CONTROL

Many years ago, our corn patch was badly infested with hordes of black aphids. Upon closer inspection, I discovered hundreds of tiny opaque eggs dangling from threadlike stalks underneath the leaves. Within days, those eggs hatched into an army of lacewing larvae, each one programmed to devour aphids. Several weeks later, the black aphids were gone, and the corn was outstanding.

We could have chosen to deal with the infestation with pesticides instead of letting nature take its course. The residential use of pesticides is epidemic in the United States. Each year, over 60 million birds die from either direct or indirect exposure to the millions of pounds of pesticides used. That needn't be the case. There are safer alternatives to growing a healthy lawn and garden.

First of all, before you take any control measures, you need to accept the fact that a few pest insects are a natural and essential part of any healthy habitat. Only when the ecosystem gets out of balance—an imbalance that can result from persistent pesticide use—do pest insects become abundant enough to cause any significant damage to plants.

If pests do get out of hand, try giving nature a chance. Among your most valuable allies when trying to keep pests in check are beneficial bugs, insects such as the lacewing, lady beetle, brown- or black-striped syrphid fly, praying mantis, dragonfly, and damselfly. They play a vital role in maintaining a finely tuned ecosystem in both natural and backyard habitats.

How so? These hard-working insects devour pests that threaten to defoliate the landscape. For example, lady beetles not only feed on aphids, but they also relish mites, mealy bugs, and the eggs of other pests. And the praying mantis emerges each spring to eat mosquitoes, beetles, flies, grasshoppers, crickets, and spiders. While some adult beneficials prey on insects (the praying mantis and the dragonfly do so exclusively), it's mostly the larvae that consume hordes of pests.

Remember, beneficial bugs don't just act as a very efficient means of organic pest control. These insects also do double duty as effective pollinators. And sometimes they even become a satisfying meal for hungry birds.

Ground Covers & VINES

Whether blanketing the ground or creating lofty layers of foliage, ground covers and vines have important roles to play in your wildlife garden.

Ground covers are usually low-maintenance perennial plants that add beauty to the garden whether they're planted under a tree or they're acting as a stabilizer on a steep slope where little else grows. Some form virtually flat mats measuring 6 inches high at most while others mature into low, arching branches of dense foliage. Certain ground covers multiply by underground runners or rooting stems that spread; others form closely spaced clumps. They come in a wide range of colors, textures, shapes, and sizes, often featuring flowers that, when planted in masses, grow into a dazzling tapestry.

When it comes to wildlife, ground covers furnish birds, butterflies and beneficial insects with shelter, along with tempting food in the form of nectar, fruit, and seeds. Moths feed on the nectar as well. Grasses and sedges—pennisetum, for example—can serve as host plants for butterfly eggs and caterpillars.

Vines can be either fast-growing annuals, such as morning glory or moonflower, or longer-lasting

Groundcovers & Vines*

CARPET BUGLE

CARPET BUGLE *(Ajuga* spp.**)*
Zones/Regions: Zones 3 to 10; all regions.

Excellent ground cover, with about 50 species of low-growing perennials and annuals; flowers in shades of pink, purple, and lavender-blue, with foliage on some species tinged chocolate, purple, or variegated with tints of pink or white. Grows as mat-forming or spreading carpets from 4 to 16 inches; easy to grow in full sun to partial shade and slightly moist soil.

Wildlife Uses: Flowers (nectar), seeds, insects; attracts butterflies and hummingbirds with nectar, insects and seeds attract ground-feeding birds, including wrens, towhees, and juncos; flowers also attract beneficial insects.

AVOID INVASIVES

Check with your county extension office or the USDA's Invasive Species website (www.invasivespecies.gov) for plants to avoid in your particular area.

Here are some perennials and vines you'll probably want to avoid:

PERENNIALS
Purple loosestrife *(Lythrum salicaria)*
Canadian thistle *(Cirsium arvense)*
Japanese knotweed
   (Polygonum cuspidatum)
Leafy spurge *(Euphorbia esula)*

VINES
Japanese honeysuckle
   (Lonicera japonica)
Kudzu *(Pueraria lobata)*
Purple crown vetch *(Coronilla varia)*
Oriental bittersweet
   (Celastrus orbiculatus)

perennials, such as the lady bank's rose or clematis. Like ground covers, vines also supply winged wildlife with necessities such as shelter, as well as valuable nesting sites and materials. What's especially beneficial is that most vines are flowering plants; in particular, many offer easily accessible nectar, a berry buffet, or insects for hungry wildlife. Female butterflies use vines such as bean plants as nurseries for their young.

In addition to being an attractive addition to the garden—especially in a young landscape waiting to fill in—vines are versatile because their flexible stems are quite willing to bend in any direction. That makes them ideal for growing horizontally across walls and vertically up any structure or element, whether encircling a post, growing up a tree, or weaving through a fence. Keep in mind that any vine will decelerate its growth when left to deal with less than adequate conditions. Speed its development along by not skimping on any of the growing essentials, especially water. Give perennials an extra dose of tender loving care the first year or two until they get their roots firmly established in the ground.

HONEYSUCKLE

Honeysuckle *(Lonicera* spp.)
Zones/Regions: Zones 2 to 11; all regions.

Group of deciduous and evergreen twining climbers with at times highly fragrant tubular or trumpet-shaped flowers; summer bloom ranging in color from pale yellow to orange to red, with colors deepening after bloom opens; followed by red or purple berries in fall; tolerates a wide range of growing conditions; best grown in full sun to partial shade.

Wildlife Uses: Flowers (nectar), berries, shelter, nesting sites and material; attracts berry-eating birds, including robins, bluebirds, towhees and waxwings; nectar-rich flowers appeals to orioles, hummingbirds, moths, and other insects; also attracts butterflies, including swallowtails and skippers.

*See page 42 for map showing zones and regions.
***Spp.* is the abbreviation for the plural of *species*.

61

HOPS

HOPS *(Humulus lupulus)*
Zones/Regions: Zones 4 to 10; all regions except colder parts of MW and CD.

Climbing perennial vine with coarsely toothed leaves; small, drooping, fragrant flowers appear in summer, followed by peculiar conelike fruit (known as strobiles) emerging in fall; very attractive when grown over an arbor, pergola, or gazebo. Best grown in full sun in moist, well-drained, and fertile soil.

Wildlife Uses: Flowers (nectar), fruit, leaves, shelter; attracts bees and other beneficial insects as well as birds; caterpillar host plant for anglewings, red admirals, hairstreaks, mourning cloaks, and spring azures.

HOSTA

HOSTA *(Hosta spp.)*
Zones/Regions: Zones 5 to 10; NW, NE, SW, SE; warmer parts of MW and CD.

More than 2,000 named cultivars with funnel-shaped flowers—some fragrant—emerging atop clump-forming leaves; size ranges from petite to colossal, with leaves colored in surprising shades of blue, vibrant yellow, chartreuse, soft cream, and seafoam to emerald green; varied leaf shape and size, which can be puckered, ruffled, ribbed, or smooth. Grows 10 inches to 6 feet, with best growth occurring in partial to full shade and average water.

Wildlife Uses: Flowers (nectar), insects, shelter; attracts insects that wrens, towhees, and other ground-feeding birds relish; nectar-rich flowers appeal to hummingbirds.

IVY

IVY *(Hedera spp.)*
Zones/Regions: Zones 4 to 10; all regions except colder parts of MW and CD.

Efficient ground covers that blanket the earth or grow upright, clinging to walls, fences, or trees by aerial roots; leaf shapes vary from typical ivy shape to curly, fan, or heart-shaped, with colors in shades of green, yellow, or variegated tones of green, yellow, pink, or cream; insignificant flowers borne in clusters and followed by berries. Grows in almost any soil from full shade to full sun, with plants in hot climates requiring some shade.

Wildlife Uses: Flowers, berries, shelter, nesting sites; attracts pollinating insects and ground-feeding birds; also attracts berry-feeding birds, including cardinals, finches, and towhees.

MORNING GLORY

MORNING GLORY *(Ipomoea spp.)*
Zones/Regions: Zones 8 to 12; all regions.

Annual, self-seeding vines with dazzling, trumpet-shaped summer flowers that range from heavenly blues, soft lavenders, and rich purples to scarlet pinks and blazing reds; grows as a perennial in frost-free climates; individual flowers bloom for only one day, with most species opening their flowers in the morning; moonflower (*I. alba*) opens its white flowers at dusk. Grows in full sun and needs ample water during the growing season.

Wildlife Uses: Flowers (nectar), shelter, nesting material; attracts hawk and sphinx moths along with other insects, including lady beetles and syrphid flies; spent vines also attract nesting birds.

SWEET ALYSSUM

SWEET ALYSSUM *(Lobularia maritima)*
Zones/Regions: Zones 7 to 10; all regions.

Frost-hardy annuals or short-lived perennials with honey-scented flowers in white, cream, and pastel shades of rose, pink, and lavender; compact mounds of tiny flowers form rounded heads that bloom from spring until frost; year-round in temperate climates; often self-seeding, grows up to 10 inches tall; easily grown in full sun but will tolerate light shade.

Wildlife Uses: Flowers (nectar); attracts butterflies and beneficial insects, especially bees and syrphid flies.

VIRGINIA CREEPER

VIRGINIA CREEPER
(Parthenocissus quinquefolia)
Zones/Regions: Zones 3 to 10; all regions.

North American native with attractive compound leaves that turn a brilliant scarlet red in fall; self-clinging perennial climber that bears insignificant flowers in summer followed by small blue-black berries in late summer or fall. Grows in sun or shade; best when grown in filtered light and humus-rich, well-drained soil.

Wildlife Uses: Flowers (nectar), fruit, shelter; attracts warblers, robins, thrushes, wrens, and other birds seeking shelter or berries; nectar-rich flowers attract small bees and other beneficial insects.

Sample Garden Plans

NIGHT-BLOOMING MOTH GARDEN

Nocturnal creatures with a good sense of smell, moths are especially attracted to flowers that bloom and exude their fragrance at night. Here's a design for a relatively simple front entry garden that combines container and flowerbed plantings along with garden accessories. It features various colors, textures, and forms for a garden that's certainly attractive by day. But it really comes alive at night when nocturnal flowers open and day-blooming nectar flowers such as honeysuckle or petunias become more fragrant. Their scent fills the night air, and showy moths come out from undercover. The basic design can accommodate any entry—just adjust the size of the flowerbed and the number of plants, hanging baskets, and containers.

MATERIALS

2 wall trellises

Stone, brick, or wood for edging flowerbed

Planting soil* and potting mix

Plants**

Bench

Large decorative pot

3 hanging baskets to be planted with trailing petunias and evening-scented stock

Plant hangers or hooks

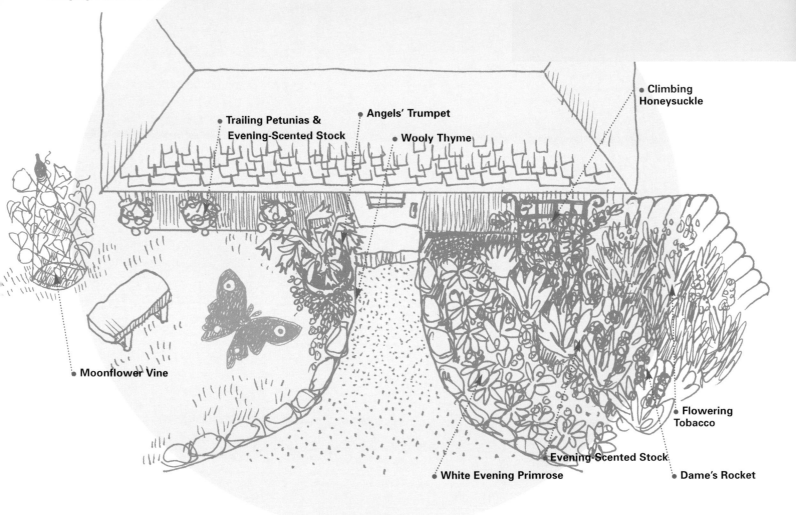

Trailing Petunias & Evening-Scented Stock

Angels' Trumpet

Wooly Thyme

Climbing Honeysuckle

Moonflower Vine

White Evening Primrose

Evening-Scented Stock

Flowering Tobacco

Dame's Rocket

TOOLS

Garden hose, heavy rope, or powdered limestone for marking the flowerbed

* You can use a blend of three parts garden soil with one part compost.

** Night-blooming moth plants as follows:

1 climbing honeysuckle
3 flowering tobacco
7 dame's rockets
9 white evening primrose
1 moonflower vine
1 angels' trumpet
3 woolly thyme
1-3 evening-scented stock per basket, depending on basket's size
3-5 trailing petunias per basket, depending on the basket's size

A luna moth alights on a lantana.

INSTRUCTIONS

I. To create the flowerbed, use the garden hose, heavy rope, or powdered limestone to mark out an area appropriate to your entry. Remove any sod or debris. Install the wall trellis within the borders of the bed and up against the house. Build a curved and raised bed, edge with stone, brick, or wood, and then fill with a good loamy planting soil.

2. First, plant the honeysuckle directly in front of the trellis. Next, arrange plants in the flowerbed as shown in the illustration, and then plant, making sure to stagger plants of the same type so they're not lined up in straight rows like soldiers.

3. Install a trellis at the other corner of the house and plant the moonflower vine directly in front of it. Place a bench nearby.

4. Plant angels' trumpet in a decorative pot and plant the area around the pot with woolly thyme. Place by the front door. By moonlight, the silvery foliage will appear almost fluorescent, casting an illuminating effect beneath the angels' trumpet.

5. If you're using smaller 8- to 10-inch baskets, plant one evening-scented stock in the middle and surround it with three trailing petunias. For baskets with diameters of 12 or more inches, plant three evening-scented stocks and five trailing petunias. Hang the baskets between the potted angels' trumpets and the moonflower trellis; you can either hang the baskets from hooks underneath the house eaves or from plant hangers attached to the wall. Be sure to stagger the height of each basket to create additional interest.

Honeysuckle

PLANT KEY FOR THE NIGHT-BLOOMING MOTH GARDEN

Many of these plants grow as perennials only in warmer regions of the country. But even in colder zones that experience frost, these self-seeders will keep coming back season after season. All of these plants become more fragrant at night.

CLIMBING HONEYSUCKLE *(Lonicera spp.*)*: Perennial vine with tubular flowers. Grows in full sun to partial shade.

FLOWERING TOBACCO *(Nicotiana sylvestris)*: Self-seeding tender perennial with tubular white flowers. Very drought-tolerant; grows from 4½ to 7 feet in full sun to partial shade.

WHITE EVENING PRIMROSE *(Oenothera caespitosa)*: Low mounding perennial with summer-blooming white flowers that open in the evening. Drought tolerant; grows from 8 to 12 inches high in full sun to partial shade.

*Spp. is the abbreviation for the plural of species.

DAME'S ROCKET

(Hesperis matronalis): Short-lived hardy perennial that replants by self-seeding; clusters of late spring to summer flowers in white or lilac. Grows from 2 1/2 to 3 feet in full sun or light shade.

EVENING-SCENTED STOCK

(Matthiola longipetala): Summer-flowering annual with creamy yellow, pink, or white flowers. Grows from 12 to 15 inches in full sun to light shade.

MOONFLOWER VINE

(Ipomoea alba): Grows as a tender perennial in frost-free zones and as a self-seeding annual in most of North America. Climbing vine grows to 20 feet, with white saucer-shaped flowers that open at night. Grows in full sun.

ANGELS' TRUMPET

(Brugmansia spp.): Small tree that grows from 5 to 10 feet tall in large containers; a mass of drooping, tubular flowers up to 8 inches long; powerfully fragrant at night and in the early morning hours. In areas where it frosts, overwinter potted plants indoors, and water sparingly through winter. Grows in full sun to partial shade.

WOOLLY THYME

(Thymus pseudolanuginosus): Hardy perennial with pink summer flowers that spill over sides of containers; silvery mat of woolly leaves growing from 1 to 3 inches high; seems to glow under moonlight. Grows in full sun to light shade.

TRAILING PETUNIAS *(Petunia* x *hybrida)*: Fast-growing annuals that tumble over hanging baskets; small funnel-shaped flowers. Best grown in full sun.

NIGHT-BLOOMING MOTH GARDEN VARIATIONS

For a different look, create several beds and locate the garden in an area of your yard near silver or gray-leaved trees, such as weeping silver pear tree *(Pyrus salicifolia)*, Russian olive *(Elaeagnus angustifolia)*, or eucalyptus *(Eucalyptus spp.)*. Additional moth-attracting plants include datura *(Datura* spp.*)*, Chilean jasmine *(Mandevilla laxa)*, yucca *(Yucca* spp.*)*, night-scented jessamine *(Cestrum nocturnum)*, evening star *(Mentzelia laevicaulis)*, and lilac *(Syringa* spp.*)*.

A spotted towhee may opt for seeds, fruit, or insects—all three can be found in this spent tomato plant.

PHASING-IN THE SONGBIRD GARDEN

You can certainly replicate this songbird garden in a single season if you've got the time and resources. But if that's not the case, don't fret. Here's a three-year plan that allows you to phase-in a garden that will draw songbirds to your backyard.

YEAR ONE

Plant the trees and large shrubs: maple, American mountain ash, flowering dogwood, columnar conifers, broad upright conifer, doublefile viburnum, elder, weeping conifer, and birch. Mark out the garden beds. Install the birdbath, bird feeders, and nest boxes.

YEAR TWO

Plant the small shrubs and slow-growing perennials, vines, and ground covers: Virginia creeper, Japanese silver grass, beautyberry, viburnum, daphne, fragrant sumac, Japanese spirea, spirea, cotoneaster, ground cover juniper, blue oat grass, wintercreeper, zinnias, and globe thistle. Create lawn and paths. Carve out and install the log and dust bath niche.

YEAR THREE

Plant all remaining plants: catmint, Bowles' golden sedge, blue fescue, purple coneflower, bellflower, dwarf aster, goldenrod, blanket flower, little bluestem, ornamental millet, amaranth, borage, black-eyed Susan, creeping St. John's wort, and showy sedum. Fill in the rest of the ground covers for the dust bath and the bench/birdbath niches. Plant pocket fillers in empty spaces around the border edges. Add a bench, table, and chairs.

SONGBIRD GARDEN

Here's a plan that allows you to put all that you've learned so far about attracting wildlife into practice. The free-flowing design for this 44 x 33-foot garden makes the most of a small space. It incorporates creature features designed to attract a wide variety of songbirds throughout the year, along with plantings that demonstrate the principles of diversity and wildlife zoning. You'll be able to meet wildlife's basic needs by offering a veritable buffet of berries, seeds, and flowers, along with evergreen and deciduous trees that provide shelter, perching, and nesting sites. Strategically placed birdbaths and feeders supply water for drinking and bathing as well as additional food sources. Amenities also include a dust bath, along with a fallen tree limb where hungry nuthatches, brown creepers, and other insect feeders can uncover a treasure trove of tunneling insects and grubs.

Of course, no bird sanctuary is complete without a meandering path for leisurely walks and cozy seating for bird watching—everything you need to enjoy a beautiful landscape and the wildlife show. Best of all, you can adapt the design to almost any size space, large or small, simply by increasing the number of plants within a group or by using some of the groupings while paring down others.

PLANT KEY FOR THE SONGBIRD GARDEN

Here is a list of plants for the songbird garden. I've listed options under each numbered plant (both species belonging to the same genus and different plants altogether). All of these plants are suitable for all regions. Of course, if you want advice about which species will work best in your area, ask the staff at your local nursery or garden center.

1. WINTERCREEPER
(Euonymus fortunei); 1 to 2 feet

2. GLOBE THISTLE
(Echinops spp.*); 3 to 4 feet
Options: *Echinops* 'Taplow Blue', 'Veitch's Blue', or 'Blue Globe'

Sedum

3. CREEPING ST. JOHN'S WORT (*Hypericum calycinum*); 12 to 18 inches
Options: Moonbeam coreopsis, also known as thread leaf coreopsis (*Coreopsis verticillata* 'Moonbeam')

4. WEEPING CONIFERS of various species; Low, pendulous habit
Options: Weeping Norway spruce (*Picea abies* 'Pendula') or weeping Colorado blue spruce (*P. pungens* 'Procumbens'); weeping Japanese red pine (*Pinus densiflora* 'Pendula') or weeping Eastern white pine (*P. strobus* 'Pendulous'); weeping Canada hemlock (*Tsuga canadensis* 'Cole's Prostrate')

5. BOWLES' GOLDEN SEDGE (*Carex elata* '*Aurea*'); 2 feet
Options: Japanese forest grass (*Hakonechloa macra* 'Aureola')

6. CATMINT (*Nepeta* spp.); 2 feet
Options: *Nepeta racemosa* 'Walker's Low' or *N.* x *faassenii* 'Dropmore' or 'Blue Wonder'

7. SPIREA (*Spiraea* spp.); 2 feet
Options: Bridal wreath spirea (*Spiraea nipponica* 'Snowmound') or Japanese spirea (*S. japonica* 'Magic Carpet' or '*Shirobana*)

8. JAPANESE SPIREA (*Spiraea japonica*); 3 to 4 feet
Options: *Spiraea japonica* 'Goldmound', 'Little Princess', or 'Neon Flash'

9. BLUE FESCUE (*Festuca glauca*); 1 foot
Options: *Festuca glauca* 'Elijah Blue' or 'Siskiyou Blue'

10. PURPLE CONEFLOWER (*Echinacea purpurea*); 2 to 3 feet

11. BELLFLOWER (*Campanula* spp.); 3 to 5 feet
Options: Milky bellflower (*Campanula lactiflora*) or giant bellflower (*C. latifolia*)

12. DWARF ASTER; 18 to 24 inches (*Aster* spp.)
Options: Italian aster (*Aster amellus*), *A.* x *frikartii*, or New England aster (*A. novae-angliae* 'Purple Dome')

13. COTONEASTER (*Cotoneaster* spp.); 2 to 3 feet
Options: Cranberry cotoneaster (*Cotoneaster apiculatus*) or rockspray cotoneaster (*C. horizontalis*)

14. BLANKET FLOWER (*Gaillardia* x *grandiflora*); 1 to 2 feet

15. BORAGE (*Borago officinalis*); 2 to 3 feet (self-seeding annual)

16. AMARANTH (*Amaranthus* spp.); 3 to 4 feet (annual)
Options: Love-lies-bleeding (*Amaranthus caudatus*), purple amaranth (*A. cruentus*), or Joseph's coat (*A. tricolor*)

17. GOLDENROD (*Solidago* spp.); 3 feet
Options: *Solidago* 'Crown of Rays', 'Goldenmosa', or 'Fireworks'

18. BIRCH (*Betula* spp.); 12 to 18 feet
Options: Water birch (*Betula occidentalis*) or dwarf river birch (*B. nigra* 'Little King'); weeping pussy willow (*Salix caprea* 'Pendula')

19. BLUE OAT GRASS (*Helictotrichon sempervirens*); 2 to 3 feet

20. LITTLE BLUESTEM (*Schizachyrium scoparium*); 2 feet
Options: Gayfeather (*Liatris spicata* 'Kobold')

21. BLACK-EYED SUSAN (*Rudbeckia hirta, R. fulgida*); 2 to 3 feet
Options: *Rudbeckia* 'Goldsturm Strain', 'Prairie Sun', or 'Indian Summer'

22. ZINNIAS (*Zinnia angustifolia, Z. elegans*); 1 to 2 feet (annual)

23. ORNAMENTAL MILLET 'Purple Majesty' (*Pennisetum glaucum* 'Purple Majesty'); 3 to 5 feet (annual)
Options: Broom corn (*Panicum miliaceum*)

24. JAPANESE SILVER GRASS (*Miscanthus sinensis*); 5 to 6 feet
Options: *Miscanthus sinensis* 'Adagio', 'Morning Light', or 'Silver Feather'

25. GROUND COVER JUNIPER (*Juniperus* spp.); spreading to 2 feet tall
Options: Chinese juniper (*Juniperus chinensis* 'Daub's Frosted'), *J. horizontalis* 'Mother Lode', or *J. squamata* 'Blue Star'

Spirea

26. SHOWY SEDUM

(*Sedum spectabile*); 12 to 18 inches
Options: *Sedum* 'Ruby Glow', 'Vera Jameson', 'Ruby Jewel'; pincushion flower (*Scabiosa columbaria* 'Butterfly Blue' or 'Pink Mist')

27. BROAD UPRIGHT CONIFER (of various types of trees); 8 to 10 feet

Options: Dwarf Colorado blue spruce (*Picea pungens* 'Montgomery'); dwarf pine (*Pinus contorta* 'Taylor's Sunburst' or *P. thunbergii* 'Thunderhead'); Chinese juniper (*Juniperus chinensis* 'Pyramidalis')

28. VIRGINIA CREEPER (*Parthenocissus quinquefolia*); deciduous vine

29. BEAUTYBERRY

(*Callicarpa americana*); 3 to 5 feet
Options: Red chokeberry (*Aronia arbutifolia*) or black chokeberry (*A. melanocarpa*)

30. MAPLE (*Acer* spp.); 30 to 40 feet

Options: hedge maple (*Acer campestre*), paperbark maple (*A. griseum*), or red maple (*A. rubrum* 'Autumn Blaze', 'Gerling', 'October Glory')

31. FLOWERING DOGWOOD

(*Cornus florida*); 10 to 15 feet
Options: Pagoda dogwood (*Cornus alternifolia*); witch hazel (*Hamamelis* x *intermedia* or *H. japonica* x *H. mollis*)

32. AMERICAN MOUNTAIN ASH

(*Sorbus americana*) or European mountain ash (*S. aucuparia*);
25 to 35 feet
Options: White (*Morus alba*), Indian (*M. indica*), or red mulberry (*M. rubra* 'Illinois Everbearing')
Note: Grow clematis or climbing hydrangea (*Hydrangea anomala petiolaris*) up the tree.

33. DOUBLEFILE VIBURNUM

(*Viburnum plicatum tomentosum*); 6 to 8 feet
Options: *Viburnum plicatum tomentosum* 'Shasta', 'Mariesii', or 'Summer Snowflake'; winter honeysuckle (*Lonicera fragrantissima*) or *Lonicera ledebourii*

34. FRAGRANT SUMAC

(*Rhus aromatica*); 3 to 4 feet
Options: Rugosa rose (*Rosa rugosa*)

35. VIBURNUM

(*Viburnum* spp.); 3 to 4 feet
Options: Arrow-wood (*Viburnum dentatum* 'Blue Muffin') or dwarf European viburnum (*V. opulus* 'Compactum'); rugosa rose (*Rosa rugosa*)

36. COLUMNAR CONIFERS

(of various types of trees); 15 to 25 feet
Options: Irish juniper (*Juniperus communis* 'Stricta') or pencil cedar (*J. virginiana* 'Blue Arrow'); American arborvitae (*Thuja occidentalis* 'Smaragd' or 'Emerald')

37. DAPHNE

(*Daphne* spp.); 3 to 4 feet
Options: February daphne (*Daphne mezereum*) or *D.* x *burkwoodii* 'Carol Mackie' or 'Somerset'

38. ELDER (*Sambucus* spp.);

8 to 10 feet
Options: European red elder (*Sambucus racemosa* 'Sutherland Gold') or black elder (*S. nigra* 'Black Beauty')

GROUND COVER OPTIONS

for dust bath niche:
Woolly yarrow (*Achillea tomentosa*); **moss phlox** (*Phlox subulata*); **Scotch moss** (*Sagina subulata*); **creeping thyme**, also known as mother of thyme (*Thymus serpyllum*).

GROUND COVER OPTIONS

for bench/birdbath niche:
Carpet bugleweed (*Ajuga reptans*); **moss phlox** or **creeping phlox** (*Phlox subulata*); **Scotch moss** (*Sagina subulata*); or **chameleon plant** (*Houttuynia cordata*).

POCKET FILLERS FOR EMPTY SPACES around border edges:

Carpet bugle bugleweed (*Ajuga reptans*); **low-growing sedum** (*Sedum* spp.); or **blue fescue** (*Festuca glauca*).

*Spp. is the abbreviation for the plural of *species*.

Chapter 5

Two owl butterflies dine on fruit at a feeding station situated near a drift of flowering star clusters. Note the owl-like eyespots located on the undersides of the hindwings, a characteristic marking of this butterfly.

PROVIDING FOOD

As essential as it is to provide the right mix of plants and year-round water sources to attract wildlife to your yard, supplying a few extra amenities can make the difference between inviting them to stop over briefly or having them linger. Offering extra food can go a long way toward creating a complete wildlife haven. Read on, and you'll find detailed instructions for building a variety of feeders.

A scrub jay pauses for a moment at a feeder.

Feeder BASICS

Other than the sugar water used to fill the hummingbird feeder, you'll generally be stocking the feeders described in this chapter with fruit, birdseed, or nuts. Overly ripe fruits supply certain butterflies—mourning cloaks, for instance—with sweet liquid, but butterflies aren't the only ones you can attract with fruit. Some birds favor fresh or dried fruit as well, along with nuts.

You'll be filling your feeders most frequently with seed. Different species prefer different seeds. You can refer to the wildlife profiles in chapter 9, as well as to A Bill of Fare for Birds on this page, if you want to know what you can set out to tempt a particular species to your yard.

A pair of evening grosbeaks takes a break from eating sunflower seeds at a tube feeder.

A BILL OF FARE FOR BIRDS

SUNFLOWER: Appeals to the widest variety of seed-eating birds, including buntings, cardinals, chickadees, crossbills, finches, goldfinches, grosbeaks, jays, juncos, mourning doves, nuthatches, pine siskins, redpolls, sparrows, tanagers, titmice, woodpeckers, and wrens.

MILLET (white proso): Buntings, cardinals, finches, goldfinches, grosbeaks, juncos, mourning doves, pine siskins, sparrows, and towhees.

SAFFLOWER: Cardinals, chickadees, finches, goldfinches, grosbeaks, mourning doves, nuthatches, and thrushes.

THISTLE (niger): Buntings, chickadees, finches, goldfinches, pine siskins, redpolls, and sparrows.

CRACKED CORN: Cardinals, finches, goldfinches, grosbeaks, jays, juncos, mourning doves, nuthatches, sparrows, titmice, towhees, warblers, and woodpeckers.

UNSALTED PEANUT KERNELS & NUTMEATS: Cardinals, chickadees, grosbeaks, jays, juncos, mourning doves, nuthatches, robins, titmice, and woodpeckers.

FRUIT: Bluebirds, cardinals, grosbeaks, mockingbirds, orioles, robins, sapsuckers, tanagers, thrashers, towhees, waxwings, woodpeckers, and wrens.

SUET: Chickadees, finches, goldfinches, grosbeaks, jays, juncos, nuthatches, robins, sparrows, thrashers, wrens, and woodpeckers.

GOING NATIVE

Wild patches in your yard can provide food for birds and offer many butterfly species a place to rest at night or take cover during bad weather. Let a corner of your yard revert back to its native roots, leave a seldom-seen portion of your lawn unmowed, or plant a mix of short and tall grasses in an out-of-the-way location. Why not establish a small-scale meadow filled with wildflowers? Just sow a pack of wildflower seeds suitable for your growing conditions.

Cloaked in muted tones of olive yellow and brown, a female American goldfinch peers up from a blueberry bush.

In general, you can avoid waste and keep your backyard flock content by keeping your seed selection simple. While inexpensive mixes are available, they often contain one or two types of seeds that birds will kick out of the way just to get to their favorites. The seed preferred by the widest variety of birds is black-oil sunflower—a high-energy, high-nutrient powerhouse. When you're trying to lure ground-feeding birds to your yard, white millet is a good choice. Scatter it on the ground, or put it in a low platform feeder. If you do opt for a specialty mix, choose one that contains mostly sunflower seeds, with fillers like millet or cracked corn.

Don't forget that moldy foods and unclean feeders can be fatal to birds. Diseases such as salmonella can spread at feeding stations, but you can put a damper on disease by keeping feeders clean and seeds dry. Start by storing seeds in an airtight container that's clean and dry. Then use a covered feeder that keeps seeds dry in wet weather. You should clean your feeders at least once a year, though more often is better if avian diseases have been a problem in the past. Scrub feeders thoroughly, using a stiff brush and 10 percent bleach solution (one part bleach to nine parts warm water), and rinse well. Make sure feeders are completely dry before refilling with seeds.

A variety of feeders placed at different heights will always attract more birds than one lone feeder that features just one birdseed. Also, offering more than one feeder helps alleviate the problem of aggressive birds taking over the feeder (see Outwitting Nuisance Birds, page 73).

In this chapter, you'll find project instructions for platform, tube, and specialty feeders. Tray or platform feeders, such as the Hanging Platform Feeder on page 78, have raised sides to keep the seeds from falling out. Placed 1 to 3 feet above the ground, they are often preferred by ground-feeding birds, such as juncos, sparrows, towhees, and mourning doves. Tube feeders like the Hanging Tube

Feeder on page 82 are long, seed-filled tubes with feeding ports and perches. While some are designed with small openings for dispensing thistle (niger) seed, favored by small birds like goldfinches, finches, pine siskins, and redpolls, others have larger openings suitable for dispensing sunflower seeds. Grosbeaks, finches, goldfinches, and chickadees will be especially attracted to this feeder/seed combination. Also included are specialty feeders—the Covered Bridge Fruit Feeder on page 75, the Fruit Tree on page 84, and the Hummingbird Feeder on page 86. They're designed for a specific site, type of feed (fruit or suet, for example), or bird species.

Feeders hanging underneath an oak tree provide both protective shelter from predator hawks and a feast for a variety of birds, including the evening grosbeak and goldfinches pictured here.

Once you've completed your feeder, you can mount it to a pole or hang it by a rope, chain, or wire from a tree branch, porch frame, or pole designed for hanging baskets or feeders. When locating bird feeders, you'll need to put them in a spot that affords birds easy access to protective cover. You can accomplish that goal by hanging them in a sheltered area at least 3 feet apart, 6 feet off the ground, and within about 10 feet of trees or shrubs. If you mount a feeder on a tree, you might want to include a baffle to keep predators at bay (see Keeping Out the Riff-Raff, page 74); a baffle is a platter-shaped or conical object that blocks access to a feeder or nest box. To make it more difficult for cats to stage an attack, consider fencing around the base of your feeder posts.

The wire cage surrounding this feeder allows entry for smaller birds like this red-breasted nuthatch, while barring access to larger, more aggressive birds.

OUTWITTING NUISANCE BIRDS

Any bird can become a nuisance when they get out of hand. For instance, blackbirds, starlings, jays, or house sparrows may bully other songbirds and take over the feeder. To cope with this situation, try selective feeding by eliminating the foods these nuisance birds seek. Or if you want to try another tack, divert their attention with a decoy feeding station that contains their favorite foods. There are also specialty feeders enclosed in wire cages that allow smaller songbirds to enter and feast while keeping larger, more aggressive birds out. You can create the same effect by surrounding your own feeder with chicken wire or large-mesh hardware cloth with holes large enough to allow smaller birds to enter.

Hawks and falcons are swift, aggressive fliers that prey on smaller birds. Two in particular—the sharp-shinned hawk and Cooper's hawk—are the raptors most likely to hunt at backyard feeders. Make your feeding station safer for songbirds by locating feeders within several feet of dense cover or hanging them from trees, so birds can quickly duck and hide if threatened. Don't forget the winter cover provided by evergreen shrubs and trees.

KEEPING OUT THE RIFF-RAFF

The feeders and nest boxes you've installed in your backyard have made the birds feel at home, but your job isn't done. You need to protect them from predators. Squirrels, if given the chance, devour the nuts and seeds you've set out in feeders. Sometimes they take over nest boxes as potential nesting sites, and they have been known to make a meal of bird eggs and fledglings. Raccoons and opossums invade nest boxes at night and eat eggs, fledglings, and occasionally adult birds, while domestic cats are an increasingly widespread threat to songbirds. Baffles are among the most effective ways to protect both feeders and nest boxes.

Designed to block access to a feeder or nest box, baffles are dome-, cone-, or tube-shaped objects that either clip directly above or below a feeder or are mounted on poles and trees. You can certainly purchase ready-made baffles—usually made of slick metal, polycarbonate, or plastic—in a variety of sizes and shapes at most bird supply stores. But you can also make them from materials easily found at a building supply store. Or you can utilize found objects and recycled items. Here are a few ideas to get you started.

• Recycle everyday objects into dome-shaped baffles: metal mixing bowls; plastic salad or popcorn bowls; an old wok or colander (minus the handles); or an upside-down plastic hanging basket. Just mount them above your feeder or nest box.

• Make a cone-shaped baffle by cutting a circular piece from a 24-inch square of galvanized metal. Next, starting at the circle's outer edge, cut out a small pie-shaped piece to the center to form the cone shape. Then cut out a small circle in the middle of this circular piece of metal to accommodate the pole. You can use brass screws or liquid steel (a metal adhesive that comes in a kit) to attach one edge of the metal to the other. Attach the baffle to the pole with anything that prevents the baffle from sliding down, such as a bolt, a couple of screws, or small blocks of wood attached to both sides of the post.

• Make a tube-shaped baffle by using a section of aluminum duct pipe or galvanized stovepipe about 24 inches long and 6 to 8 inches in diameter when bent into a circle. Cap the ends with a circle of ¼-inch-mesh hardware cloth to prevent snakes or squirrels from passing through. Place the tube-shaped baffle about 3 to 5 feet off the ground.

CONSTRUCTION TIPS

Choosing your construction materials carefully will ensure that in the process of meeting wildlife's needs, you don't inadvertently cause them harm. Always use untreated lumber when building feeders and nest boxes because treated wood can be toxic to birds. When glue is called for, be sure to use a nontoxic glue whenever possible, especially when birds are likely to peck at the surface. An exterior-grade wood glue is fine when you're simply gluing pieces of the projects together.

Likewise, make sure you only use water-based stains, paints, and protective finishes when painting feeders or nest boxes. The petrochemicals used in oil-based paints are harmful to birds if they should happen to peck on painted or stained surfaces. However, it is imperative that you leave the surfaces on which you'll be placing the food unpainted. You don't want birds consuming flakes of paint along with their feed.

Pine or fir will work just fine for your projects, though a high-resin wood such as redwood, cypress, or cedar will last longer. And remember that pieces of lumber have both a nominal and an actual dimension. So, for example, when a 1 x 6 board is first rough-sawn from a log, it does in fact measure 1 x 6. But after the board has been dried and planed, its final measurement is ¾ x 5½ inches. All project directions involving board lumber give both nominal and actual dimensions of the lumber.

And finally, always use galvanized or brass nails when building feeders or nest boxes. Likewise, use brass, zinc-coated, stainless steel, or galvanized screws to avoid rust. Be sure to drill pilot holes when using screws.

Covered Bridge Fruit Feeder

This covered bridge provides the perfect place to serve favorites such as apple or orange halves, pieces of plums or peaches, or even melon rinds. If you'd like, insert a couple of long nails up through the base of the feeder, and skewer orange halves or large pieces of fruit onto the nails, shish-kebab style.

MATERIALS

Untreated 1 x 6 board, * cut into (4) 12-inch pieces

Wood glue

¾- and 1¼-inch brad nails (for nail gun) or finishing nails (for hammer)

3 wood roofing shingles

Wood trim, 1 inch wide and ⅜ inch thick, cut as follows:

    (4) 12-inch pieces (for the sides of the tray and the peak of the roof)

    (2) 6 ¼-inch pieces (for the ends of the tray)

2 screw eyes, 1 inch long and ½ inch in diameter

Piece of chain, rope, or wire, 24 to 36 inches long (for hanging the feeder)

2 binder rings (for hanging the feeder)

Small paintbrush (for detail) and 1-inch paintbrush (for larger areas)

Exterior latex enamel paints— ivory, gold, green, orange, and brown

Paper (for template)

Assorted fruit, such as apples, oranges, and plums

TOOLS

Power saw and miter box or power miter saw

Nail gun or hammer

Electric drill with ⅛-inch bit

Pencil

*Note: The actual size of a 1 x 6 is ¾ x 5½ inches.

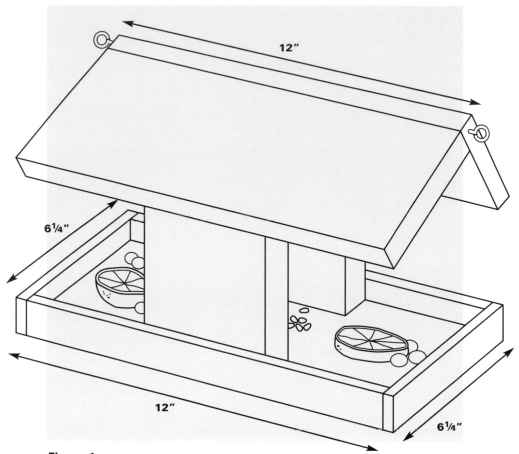

Figure 1

INSTRUCTIONS

I. To make the risers, cut one 12-inch piece of wood in half horizontally so you have two equal pieces measuring 6 inches in length. Cut a 45° angle at one end of each piece to accommodate the pitch in the roof.

2. Use wood glue and then the 1¼-inch nails to assemble the wood pieces and shingles. Use another of the 12-inch pieces for the base, and center the risers along its outer edges. Attach the risers to the bottom, making sure the beveled ends are at the top with the higher edges to the inside.

3. To make the roof, secure two of the 12-inch pieces so they form a right angle, the end of one side flush along the edge of the other (figure 2). Center the roof over the sides; it will overlap.

4. Cut the wood shingles into varying widths from 1½ to 3 inches, with the length of each piece being about 3½ inches. Begin attaching the shingles to the lower edge of the roof, and then attach the upper row so it overlaps the bottom row.

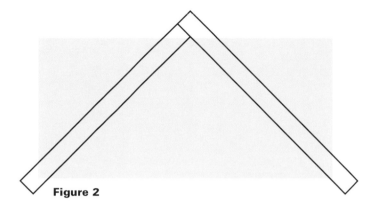

Figure 2

5. Beginning with the side pieces, glue the wood trim to the bottom, keeping the lower edges flush with the base. Secure with the ¾-inch brad nails or finishing nails.

6. Position the two pieces of trim at the peak of the shingled roof, using wood glue and ¾-inch brad nails or finishing nails to secure them.

7. Drill pilot holes at opposite ends of the roof for each of the screw eyes, as shown in figure 1. Insert both screw eyes and attach each end of the chain or wire to a screw eye, using a binder ring.

8. To decorate your feeder, paint as follows, letting the feeder dry between coats: Paint the exposed edges of the roof and the sides of the trim around the base with brown paint. Paint the top of trim around the base with gold paint. Use ivory paint on the sides, leaving the inside unpainted. (It may take two coats.)

9. Make a template for a circle that is 3⅜ inches in diameter; use a compass or a jar lid. Fold under 1 inch of the template and place the folded edge where the trim meets the riser. Trace around the circle. Fill it in with orange paint and let it dry. Use the small brush to paint a thin gold border around the orange. Finally, use the small brush and green paint to fill in the fruit segments of the design; you could also make a template for these sections if desired. Allow the paint to dry thoroughly.

10. Fill the feeder with assorted fruit and hang in your yard.

THE NITTY-GRITTY ON GRIT

Birds that eat seeds also consume small pebbles, sand, and other coarse material, commonly referred to as grit. The grit is retained in the gizzard, where it helps digestion by acting as a seed grinder. Usually outdoor birds can easily find all the grit they need, but a blanket of snow makes grit hard to find. You can help by offering grit in winter—either mixed with seeds or provided in a separate container. Grit sources include coarse sand, crushed eggshells and oyster shells, and commercial or poultry grit.

Hanging Platform Feeder

This simple and sleek platform feeder is stocked with a year-round buffet for birds. Customize your feeder with the artwork of your choice.

MATERIALS

Untreated 1 x 6 board,*
cut as follows:
  (2) 16-inch pieces
  (for the roof)
  (2) 7-inch pieces
  (for the risers)

Untreated 1 x 8 board,*
cut as follows:
  (1) 16-inch piece
  (for the bottom)

Wood glue

1½-inch brad nails (for nail gun)
or finishing nails (for hammer)

Piece of copper sheeting, at least
36-gauge, 11¾ x 16 inches

8 copper brads

Untreated ⅜ x 1-inch wood trim,
cut as follows:
  (2) 16-inch pieces
  (for the sides of the tray)
  (2) 8-inch pieces
  (for the ends of the tray)

Sandpaper

Exterior latex enamel paints—
gold and cranberry

Paper

Wax paper

Sponge

2 brass cup hooks, ⅞ inch

3 feet of brass chain

Birdseed

TOOLS

Handsaw or power saw

Pencil

Ruler

Nail gun or hammer

Small paintbrush (for detail)
and 1-inch paintbrush
(for larger areas)

Oak leaf

*Note: The actual size of a 1 x 6 is ¾ x
5½ inches; the actual size of a
1 x 8 is ¾ x 7 ¼ inches.

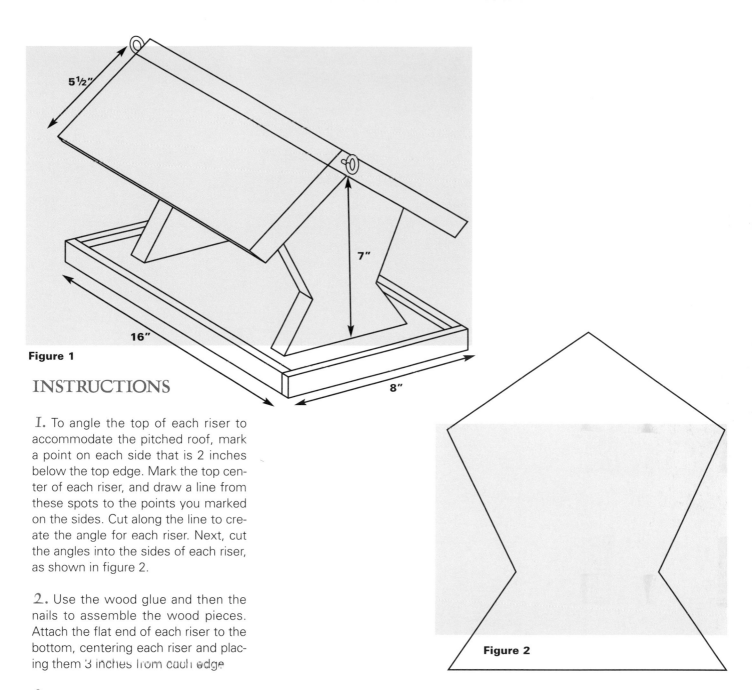

Figure 1

5½"

7"

16"

8"

Figure 2

INSTRUCTIONS

1. To angle the top of each riser to accommodate the pitched roof, mark a point on each side that is 2 inches below the top edge. Mark the top center of each riser, and draw a line from these spots to the points you marked on the sides. Cut along the line to create the angle for each riser. Next, cut the angles into the sides of each riser, as shown in figure 2.

2. Use the wood glue and then the nails to assemble the wood pieces. Attach the flat end of each riser to the bottom, centering each riser and placing them 3 inches from each edge.

3. Attach one side of the roof over the pointed risers, keeping the top edge flush with the ends of the risers. Attach the other side of the roof so its end is flush along the edge of the first side, forming a right angle. (For a detailed view of the roof, see Covered Bridge Fruit Feeder figure 2 on page 77.)

4. Bend the copper sheeting in the middle so it fits snugly over the roof. Attach the sheeting to the roof, using four copper brads on each side.

5. Beginning with the side pieces, use wood glue and nails to attach the four pieces of trim around the bottom to make a tray.

6. Sand any rough areas. Use gold paint to decorate the following: the exposed edges of the roof; the outside and exposed top edge of the trim that forms the tray; and the outside and exposed edges of the risers. Let dry and repeat with a second coat of paint.

7. Trace an oak leaf on thick paper for the template, cut it out, and trace it on the outside of each riser. Fill in the leaf with the cranberry paint. Let dry. Pour a little gold paint onto the wax paper and use the sponge to dab a little gold paint across the oak leaf. Let dry.

8. Screw a cup hook into each end of the roof and attach the brass chain. Fill with birdseed and hang.

Butterfly Fruit Feeder

Offering fruit is a great way to attract butterflies such as the monarch, mourning cloak, red-spotted purple, or tawny emperor. Once you've filled the feeder, it may take a day or two for the fruit to reach the butterfly-attracting stage—the riper the fruit, the more appealing it is to butterflies.

MATERIALS

4 clay pots, 6 inches in diameter

Clay saucer, 12 inches in diameter

Epoxy

Plastic saucer, 12 inches in diameter (optional)

Assorted overly ripe fruit and/or juice; for example: melons, berries, plums, peaches, or bananas

INSTRUCTIONS

I. To create the pedestal, place one of the pots on the ground and place a line of epoxy along the rim. Place the second pot on top of it, upside down, so the rims meet. Now glue the bottom of the third pot to the upturned bottom of the second pot, using the epoxy as described above. To complete the pedestal, add epoxy to the rim of the third pot and place the remaining pot on top of it, upside down, with the rims meeting.

2. To finish the feeder, use the epoxy to attach the bottom of the clay saucer to the top of the pedestal. When all is dry, carefully move the feeder to a sunny location in the garden where you can watch the butterflies as they feed. Bear in mind that the feeder may also attract wasps or bees, so be sure to locate it where visiting insects are welcome.

3. Fill the saucer with a variety of overly ripe fruit, like sliced bananas, peach halves, cut-up mangos, watermelon rinds, melon slices, and berries. Fill a small bowl with fermented fruit juice, pureed fruit, or leftover applesauce for an added treat. Cleanup is made easy if you either line the clay saucer with a clear or plastic saucer or serve the fruit in small bowls.

A monarch butterfly sips nectar from a buddleja flower.

A HABITAT FOR BUTTERFLIES

When offering a fruit feeder to butterflies, why not create a small-scale, multilevel habitat that provides shelter as well? Place the fruit feeder close to a tree that can serve as shelter and as a host plant for butterflies likely to visit the fruit feeder—mourning cloaks and admirals, for instance. Examples include common shelter trees like willow, aspen, elm, and birch. You can attract other types of butterflies, such as skippers and whites, by planting a middle layer of nectar sources and shelter plants like butterfly bushes or honeysuckle vines. Finish by planting nectar plants such as mallow, delphinium, wallflower, dianthus, or salvia on the lower levels.

Hanging Tube Feeder

Birds, from finches to grosbeaks, will come flocking to this large tube feeder. Its ingenious design allows both ends to open for easy cleaning. You'll use basic plumbing supplies to build this project.

MATERIALS

Piece of schedule 40 PVC pipe, 3 inches in diameter and 12 inches long

2 schedule 40 PVC female S x T (slip x thread adapters), 3 inches in diameter

Primer (for plastic)

Water-based spray paint— color of your choice

PVC glue

2 schedule 40 PVC MPT (male threaded) plugs, 3 inches in diameter

Dowel rod, ¼-inch diameter, cut into three 6-inch pieces

Piece of leather, string, or cord, ¼ inch in diameter and 36 inches long

Washer, ½ inch

Birdseed, such as sunflower seed

TOOLS

Pencil or pen

Ruler or tape measure

Electric drill with ½-inch and ¼-inch bits

Sandpaper

INSTRUCTIONS

I. To make the feeding holes, push one female S x T adapter on the bottom end of the PVC pipe. Make a mark just above the rim of the adapter, and drill a ½-inch hole at the mark, drilling completely through to the opposite side. Make another mark about 6 inches above the first hole, and drill a ½-inch hole at the second mark, again drilling through to the opposite side. To drill the third set of feeding holes, move 45° around the pipe and make a mark 3 inches above the rim of the bottom, drilling through both sides of the pipe.

2. To make the holes for the perches, make marks on both sides of the bottom adapter that are 1½ inches below the lowest feeding holes. Leave the bottom adapter on the PVC pipe and drill a ¼-inch hole through each mark. Make a mark 1½ inches below each of the remaining feeding holes, and drill a ¼-inch hole through each mark.

3. Remove the bottom adapter. Sand the PVC pipe, wipe clean, and spray with primer following the manufacturer's instructions. Let dry as directed. Paint the PVC pipe in your choice of color. Once the paint is dry, reattach the bottom S x T adapter using PVC glue. (You may wish to paint the adapters as well.)

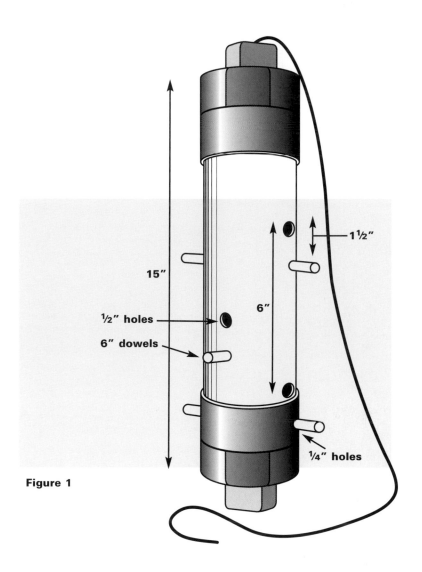

Figure 1

15"

1½"

½" holes

6" dowels

6"

¼" holes

4. Screw one of the MPT plugs to the bottom S x T adapter. Glue the remaining female S x T adapter onto the top of the feeder. Slide a 6-inch dowel through each of the ¼-inch perching holes. Secure the dowels with glue, if needed.

5. To hang the feeder, drill a ¼-inch hole through the center of the remaining MPT plug. From the top of the plug, push both ends of the leather cord through the hole. Slide the washer onto the ends of the cord and make a large knot to keep the cord from slipping through the washer and out the hole. Fill the feeder with birdseed, and screw on the top plug. Tie a knot in the cord to hang the feeder.

TIP

Sunflower seeds work best in the ½-inch diameter feeding holes. But if you prefer to cater to birds such as finches that enjoy small seeds (like thistle), make the feeding holes smaller, about ¼-inch in diameter.

ALTERNATIVE

You can also use ABS pipe and adapters for this project. (ABS is a different type of plastic used to make plumbing supplies.) Be sure you use the proper adhesive for the materials you choose, because ABS and PVC have different requirements.

Fruit Tree Feeder and Planter

What could be more appealing (or practical) than a planter that is also a feeder? Fill the planter with ground covers or low-growing flowers, such as sprawling sedums or impatiens, that will produce seeds for birds. Use branches from trees with ornamental bark—corkscrew willow or coral bark maple, perhaps—for added texture and color.

MATERIALS

- Terra-cotta flue pipe or decorative container without a bottom, 9 inches in diameter
- Tree branch, 36 to 48 inches long and 1 inch in diameter (for the trunk)
- 8 feet of 6-gauge copper wire, cut into four 2-foot pieces (for the branches)
- Plant saucer, 4 to 6 inches in diameter
- Potting mix
- 1 to 3 low-growing plants, such as thyme, blue star creeper, campanula, or sedum
- Assorted fruit, such as oranges, apples, grapes, and berries

TOOLS

- Saw
- Wire cutters
- Electric drill, bit, and screw, or exterior-grade adhesive

INSTRUCTIONS

1. Situate the flue pipe in a flowerbed or other location in the garden. Cut your branch to the desired height for your trunk; it should be between 36 and 48 inches.

2. Use the copper wire to create four branches on which to skewer the fruit. Starting at the top, wrap the first piece of wire around the trunk in a downward spiral, leaving about 12 inches free for the highest branch. Wrap each piece of wire around the trunk in a similar fashion, working your way down as you create a total of four 12-inch branches.

3. Secure the plant saucer to the top of the trunk with a screw or with the adhesive. Place the wire-wrapped trunk in the center of the flue pipe; insert the bottom of the trunk into the ground to secure. Fill the flue pipe with potting mix, packing the mix around the trunk as you fill the container.

4. To finish, fill the flue pipe with flowering plants. Skewer orange halves, apple slices, or other large pieces of fruit on the branches, and then fill the saucer with berries, grapes, or sliced bananas.

DID YOU KNOW?

Many adult moths never feed. That's because moths like the silk, yucca, and gypsy become adults for only one reason: to reproduce. Once they've mated, they perish, living for a week or so at most. In some, such as the luna moth, all vestiges of the mouth parts have actually disappeared.

Hummingbird Feeder

If you love watching hummingbirds, then you'll really enjoy the show when they swoop in for some sweet nectar from this colorful feeder. This is a great project for recycling clear glass bottles.

MATERIALS

Clear glass bottle

Frosted glass spray paint—red

Enamel spray paint—clear

5 pieces of 18-gauge silver floral wire, 18 inches long

2 binder rings, one that is ¾ inch in diameter and one big enough to slide over neck of bottle

1 cork or rubber bottle stopper (to fit the opening in bottle)

4 inches of clear plastic tubing, ¼ inch in diameter

Glass seed beads, size 5—red

1 piece of 20-gauge silver floral wire, 10 inches long

Sugar

Water

TOOLS

Wire cutters

Round-nose pliers

Electric drill with ¼-inch bit

Top of the hummingbird feeder

Flower motif

INSTRUCTIONS

I. Wash the bottle thoroughly and let dry completely. Spray with the red glass paint and let dry. Coat with at least three layers of the clear enamel spray, letting the bottle dry between coats.

2. Wrap the first piece of 18-gauge wire around the bottle, placing it about one-third of the length of the bottle. Connect the wire using a simple flower motif made with the round-nose pliers.

3. Take three of the remaining 18-gauge wires and use the pliers to make hooks on one end of each wire, forming them by creating spirals. Place the binder ring around the neck of the bottle and loop the hooks through the binder ring. Loop each of these wires around the wire you put around the bottle in step 2. Make spiral hooks at the ends of each wire; the wires should extend several inches past the bottle. Hook the ends around the ¾-inch binder ring.

4. Use the remaining piece of 18-gauge wire to fashion a loop and hanger; cut the wire into two pieces, one that is 12 inches and one that is 6 inches. Fold the 12-inch piece in half and then twist one end of the 6-inch piece around the loop to form a hanger. Make a spiral hook around the end of this wire and loop it through the ¾-inch binder ring; repeat for the ends of the 12-inch wire. You can easily remove the bottle for cleaning by detaching the wires from the binder ring.

5. Drill a ¼-inch hole all the way through the center of the bottle stopper, and then insert the plastic feeding tube into the hole until the end is almost flush with the end of the bottle. Thread the beads on the 10-inch piece of 20-gauge wire. Put a small loop in each end of the wire. Wrap the wire in a spiral around the exposed portion of the feeding tube. Bend the feeding tube into shape as in the photo.

6. Make a nectar solution using 1 part white sugar to 4 parts water. Bring the water to a boil, stir in the sugar, and lightly boil for two additional minutes. Remove from the heat and let the solution cool to room temperature, then fill the bottle feeder to three-fourths full. You can make just enough solution for one filling, or make extra to store in the refrigerator. Hang the feeder in a visible location so you can enjoy watching the hummingbirds feed.

A HABITAT FOR HUMMINGBIRDS

While hummingbirds will be drawn by the feeders you've put out for them, they'll be more likely to make your yard a favored destination if there are other nectar sources nearby. It's even better if you also include plants that offer shelter, as well as a place where hummers can bathe in water that collects on the large leaves of trees, shrubs, or perennials, like hostas. Another way to meet their need for water is to hang the feeder close to a patch of lawn. They'll enjoy bathing in the spray from the lawn sprinkler.

Here's one way to combine various levels of plantings to create your own small-scale hummingbird garden. Hang your feeder close to a tree such as a dogwood, holly, or willow tree. They'll provide shelter sites as well as nesting materials like spider webs, moss, and lichens. Then use a beauty bush as the understory, and plant the lower level with diverse plants that span the seasons: catmint and foxglove for spring, geranium and summer phlox for summer, and petunia, cleome, and salvia for the fall.

Chapter 6 SUPPLYING SHELTER

I

If you want to increase the odds that birds, dragonflies, or beneficial insects will take up permanent residence in your yard, offer them safe places to rest and reproduce. From a nesting materials box to a pipe for nonstinging orchard mason bees, that's what the projects in this chapter are designed to do.

An American robin with nesting materials in its bill

Nest Box BASICS

A nest box (otherwise known as a birdhouse) is always an open invitation to songbirds that nest in cavities rather than on the ground or in the branches of shrubs and trees. However, the box that attracts a bluebird differs markedly from one that houses a nuthatch. So the type and size of the birdhouse you put up will influence which species are likely to become your new neighbors.

Most importantly, knowing which species you'd like to attract will determine the diameter of the entrance hole you'll want to make in your nest box. As a general rule, the bigger the bird, the larger the entrance hole needs to be. You can use the wildlife profiles in chapter 9 to help you determine which species of local birds you want to coax into your yard. Both the project instructions and the wildlife profiles specify entrance hole diameters for species known to make use of nest boxes.

You can mount your nest box on a pole, a fence post, the side of an outdoor building, or on a tree trunk. The height at which you place your nest box will also affect which species will take up residence. Putting nest boxes 8 to 10 feet off the ground will suffice for most bird species, though purple martins prefer heights of 10 to 15 feet and screech owls like their boxes at heights of roughly 12 to 20 feet.

As with feeders, you'll want to take steps to keep nest boxes safe for birds. Placing the birdhouse at least 10 feet away from trees or other potential launching pads, such as the top of a building or fence, will help keep them out of the reach of predators like cats and pests such as squirrels. If predators are a problem in your area, you might also want to equip nest boxes with baffles (see Keeping Out the Riff-Raff, page 74) or guards (see Guarding Your Nest Box on page 95). Fencing around the bases of nest box posts is yet another measure you can take that might dissuade cats from attempting an attack. Protecting nest boxes from the weather needs to be another consideration when you're deciding where to put them. Choose a location that's out of direct sunlight in a protected area and make sure the entrance hole is facing away from prevailing winds.

You'll certainly want to make nest boxes available by late winter or early spring, before nesting birds arrive. That's usually by February in southern regions and by mid- to late March in northern areas. But keep in mind that nest boxes can be quite valuable during winter as well; chickadees, nuthatches, and bluebirds may occasionally take cover in them. Just be sure to clean the boxes either after each brood has departed (the ideal time) or in early spring before the new nesters arrive. All the nest box projects in this chapter have doors that swing open to make them easier to clean.

CONSTRUCTION TIPS

It's best if you use rough-sawn lumber for the interior of nest boxes, especially for the front wall. It makes it easier for young birds to climb out.

The interior of nest boxes should never be painted. You can use water-based paints, stains, or protective finishes elsewhere.

It's important that all nest boxes have adequate ventilation and drainage. Drilling a few small holes (¼ inch in diameter) in the floor will allow water to drain; several holes drilled in the sides near the top of the box will provide added ventilation.

And don't forget the lessons learned from the feeder projects in chapter 5 (page 74):

• Use untreated wood.

• Pine or fir will work, but high-resin woods such as redwood, cypress, or cedar last longer.

• Use galvanized or brass nails.

• Use brass, zinc-coated, stainless steel, or galvanized screws.

• Be sure to drill pilot holes when using screws.

• Use only water-based stains, paints, and protective finishes.

• Use nontoxic glues whenever possible, especially on surfaces birds are likely to peck. Exterior-grade wood glue can be used in other places, such as when gluing pieces of the project together.

Nesting Materials Box

This colorful resource offers a variety of nesting materials; fill it with pieces of yarn, string, dried grasses, feathers, and bits of fur. If you have a lot of nesting birds in your yard, double the dimensions to make a box that holds twice the amount of nesting materials.

MATERIALS

Untreated 1 x 6 board,* cut as follows:
  (1) 6-inch piece
  (for the sides)
  (1) 8-inch piece (for the back)
  (1) 2-inch piece
  (for the bottom)
  (1) 3¼- x 8-inch piece
  (for the top)

Wood glue

1½-inch brad nails (for nail gun) or finishing nails (for hammer)

Dowel rod, ¼ inch in diameter, cut into (3) 6¼-inch pieces

Nontoxic glue

Coconut fiber liner

Assorted nesting materials: string, yarn, dried grass, feathers, cotton balls, dryer lint, etc.

TOOLS

Handsaw or power saw

Pencil

Ruler

Electric drill with ⁵⁄₁₆-inch bit

Nail gun or hammer

*Note: The actual size of a 1 x 6 is ¾ x 5½ inches.

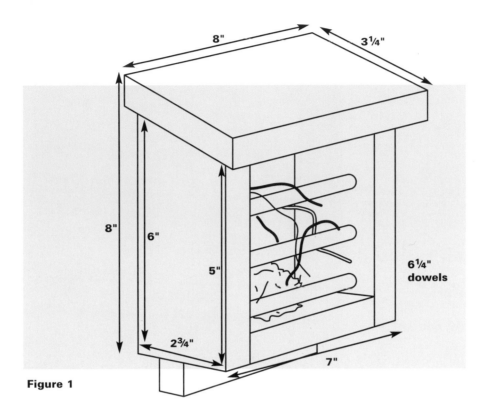

Figure 1

INSTRUCTIONS

1. Cut the 6-inch side piece in half lengthwise, leaving you with two pieces that are each 2¾ x 6 inches. Trim the top of each piece so it measures 6 inches long in back and 5 inches long in front.

2. Mark spots on the inside of each side piece to drill three ⁵⁄₁₆-inch holes for the dowels. The position of the holes must be identical on each piece. Space the marks about 1¼ inches apart, starting 1 inch from the bottom. Drill ⅜-inch-deep holes at the marks.

3. Use wood glue and then nails to assemble the wood pieces. First, attach one of the side pieces flush with the edge of the back piece; place the side piece so the back extends 1 inch below it. Next, attach the bottom by sliding it against the side and the back, keeping the bottom flush with the end of the side piece.

4. Use wood glue to secure the dowels as you place them into the holes of the constructed side. Flip the box on its side and attach the remaining side piece, putting it in place on the dowels.

5. Center the top piece over the sides and secure in place. To finish, cut a piece of coconut liner to fit the top and use the nontoxic glue to adhere it to the roof. Fill the box with assorted nesting materials.

Robin Nest Shelf

Make robins feel right at home with this custom-built nesting shelf. In fact, the open-front design can also accommodate other avian nesters such as barn swallows and phoebes.

MATERIALS

Untreated 1 x 12 board,* cut as follows:
- (1) 12-inch piece (for the top)
- (1) 9¼-inch piece (for the back)

Untreated 1 x 10 board,* cut as follows:
- (1) 9¾-inch piece (for the bottom)
- (2) 7-inch pieces (for the sides)

Wood glue

Finishing nails, ½ inch and 1½ inch

220-grit sandpaper

Water-based pre-stain wood conditioner

Water-based wood stain, color of your choice

Water-based protective finish, clear satin

Rags (for staining)

TOOLS

Handsaw or power saw

Pencil

Ruler

Hammer

Synthetic bristle brush

*Note: The actual size of a 1 x 10 is ¾ x 9¼; the actual size of a 1 x 12 is ¾ x 11¼.

INSTRUCTIONS

1. To make the angle in the side pieces, measure halfway down the front of each side, and then mark a point that is 2½ inches toward the center of each piece. Draw a line from the top and bottom corner to the mark, and then cut along the line. Repeat for the other side piece.

2. Use wood glue and then finishing nails to assemble the pieces. First, attach the side pieces to the back piece, using three nails per side.

3. Attach the bottom by sliding it between the sides and against the back. Secure using three nails per side and four nails along the back. Then, position the top piece over the back and the sides, attaching with three nails along the back and each side.

4. To prepare for finishing, sand and wipe clean. Staining and finishing the inside is optional, but if you do choose to stain the inside, be sure that the nesting shelf's floor is left unstained.

5. Follow the manufacturer's directions to apply the pre-stain wood conditioner and the wood stain. Let dry two hours and apply a second coat of stain. Let dry for three hours.

6. Follow the manufacturer's directions to apply the protective finish and let dry.

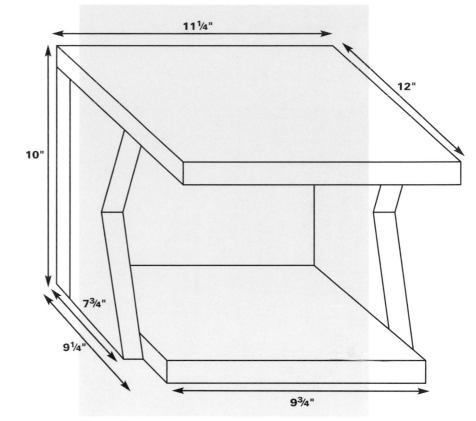

Figure 1

OFFERING BIRDS
A PACKAGE DEAL

You've finished the project and made a box that offers a ready supply of nesting materials. Now you need to offer sources of food and shelter nearby to complete the package.

• Hang the box on a tree that offers shelter and nesting sites, such as a maple, hawthorn, poplar, cottonwood, aspen, or pine.

• Include a vine that provides shelter and/or a nesting site, such as Virginia creeper, Boston ivy, winter creeper, jasmine, hops, climbing rose, or climbing hydrangea.

• Plant a small bed of seed-bearing perennials like coreopsis, black-eyed Susans, asters, and pincushion flowers, or annuals like marigolds, sunflowers, and amaranth.

• Include a nearby water source to attract flying insects for wrens, swallows, and other nesting birds whose diet consists of insects.

Enclosed Nest Box

Bark and moss mimic the appearance of a natural cavity in a tree.
Placing sawdust or wood chips in the bottom of the box may convince a
pair of chickadees that the box is indeed a newly excavated hole.

MATERIALS

Untreated 1 x 8 board,* cut as
follows:
   (4) 9-inch pieces (for the
   sides, front, and top)
   (1) 12-inch piece
   (for the back)
   (1) 5 ¾-inch piece
   (for the bottom)

Wood glue

1½-inch brad nails (for nail gun)
or finishing nails (for hammer)

Exterior-grade adhesive

Small stones

Sheet moss or moss collected
from trees

Pieces of bark and twigs

TOOLS

Handsaw or power saw

Electric drill with 1½-inch bit

Nail gun or hammer

*Note: The actual size of a
1 x 8 is ¾ x 7 ¼ inches.

INSTRUCTIONS

I. Drill a 1½-inch hole on the front, positioning the bit 2½ inches below the top.

2. Use wood glue and then nails to assemble the wood pieces. First, attach the sides to the back so they're centered along the back.

3. Attach the bottom by sliding it between the sides and against the back, keeping the bottom flush with the ends of the side pieces.

4. To attach the front, slide it between the sides. Do not glue; secure with one nail in each side, placed 1½-inches below the top. This construction allows the front door to swing open from the bottom to facilitate cleaning the box. Next, attach the top to the sides.

5. Apply a thin coat of exterior-grade adhesive around the entrance hole and press the stones into the adhesive. Apply another thin coat of adhesive or wood glue to the top and sides and cover with bark pieces. Use nails to secure if needed. Randomly glue moss around the bark.

6. Attach moss to the remaining wood surfaces, if desired. For added visual interest, nail or glue several twigs on the moss-covered front.

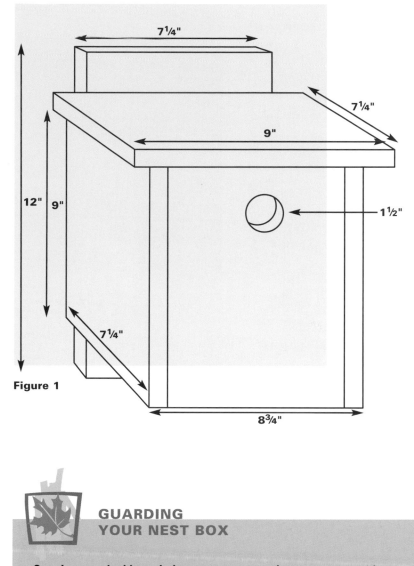

Figure 1

GUARDING YOUR NEST BOX

Guards are valuable tools in your quest to make sure your nest boxes are secure places where birds can tend to their offspring. Entrance guards protect a nest box's hole by preventing potential predators from chewing the hole so it's large enough for them to gain access. You can buy metal guards—or you can make your own. To protect a nest box, cut a hole the same size and shape as the entrance hole in the middle of a rectangular piece of sheet metal. Align the hole in the sheet metal with the box's entrance hole and attach, using finishing nails, brad nails from a staple gun, or exterior-grade construction adhesive. You can also use a guard to predator-proof a tree trunk or wooden pole by simply wrapping a 2-foot-wide band of galvanized metal or aluminum flashing so that the guard's bottom is placed a few feet above the ground.

Pitched Roof Nest Box

This is no mere birdhouse. Paint this cozy chalet to match your own home's color scheme, or shop for complementary colors at your local paint store.

MATERIALS

Untreated 1 x 6 board,*
cut as follows:
    (2) 8-inch pieces
    (for the front and back)
    (2) 6-inch pieces (for the sides)
    (2) 9-inch pieces (for the roof)
    (1) 4-inch piece (for the bottom)

Wood glue

1½-inch brad nails (for nail gun) or finishing nails (for hammer)

Forked branch, ¼ inch in diameter and 2 inches long

Exterior-grade construction adhesive

L-hook (optional)

220-grit sandpaper

Primer (optional)

Exterior latex enamel paints—colors to match your home

Cardstock (for template)

TOOLS

Handsaw or power saw

Pencil

Ruler

Electric drill with 1¼-inch bit and ¼-inch bit

Nail gun or hammer

Small paintbrush (for detail) and 1-inch paintbrush (for larger areas)

Craft scissors

*Note: The actual size of a 1 x 6 is ¾ x 5½ inches.

INSTRUCTIONS

I. To make the diagonal pitch on both the front piece and the back piece, measure and mark a point 2 inches down each side. Measure and mark the midpoint of the top, and cut each piece from the mark on the top edge to the marks on each side. Next, drill the entrance hole on the front piece 3 inches below the pointed top, using the 1¼-inch bit. (An entrance hole this size will admit chickadees, nuthatches, and titmice; if you want to limit the tenants to chickadees, make the hole's diameter 1⅛ inches.)

2. Use wood glue and then nails to assemble the wood pieces. First, attach the front and back piece to one side so the bottoms of each piece are flush. Next, attach the bottom piece.

3. Slide the remaining side between the front and back piece. To allow this side to swing open from the bottom, secure with only one nail through the front piece and one nail through the back piece, positioning both nails 1 inch below the top edge.

4. Secure one side of the roof over the angled edges of the front and the back, keeping its edge flush with the pointed ends of the front and the back. The roof should be centered over the front and the back. Attach the other side of the roof so its end is flush along the edge of the first side, forming a right angle.

5. Add the decorative perch by drilling a ¼-inch hole through the front, about 1½ inches below and to the right of the entrance hole. Coat the end of the forked branch with the construction adhesive and insert it into the hole. If desired, secure the side that opens with an L-hook.

6. Sand the box and wipe clean.

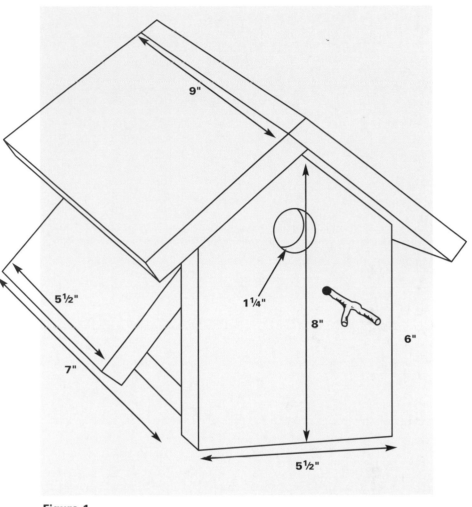

Figure 1

7. If desired, paint the exterior with primer and let dry. Paint in your chosen colors using the photo on page 96 as a guide, beginning with the walls, then the underside and edges of the roof. Paint the roof itself and let it dry.

8. If desired, make a U-shaped template that is 1 x 1 inch for the shingles, and trace it onto the roof, staggering the placement of each row.

9. Use the small brush to paint over the pencil lines and let dry. Paint a ¼-inch-wide line on each side of the peak of the roof and let dry.

DID YOU KNOW?

The male house wren will build several nests—up to a dozen or more—in hopes of having one that appeals to a female. Holding true to the familiar saying, "if you want something done right, you've got to do it yourself," the female will then select a nest and frequently throws out much of the material in the process of rebuilding the nest herself.

Chickadee Winter Roost Box

This communal roost provides a warm winter home for chickadees that don't migrate to warmer climates.

MATERIALS

Hardwood dowel rod, ½-inch diameter, cut into three 5-inch pieces

Sandpaper, 60-grit and 220-grit

Untreated 1 x 8 board,* cut as follows:
- (1) 16-inch piece (for the back)
- (3) 12-inch pieces (for the front and the sides)
- (1) 5½-inch piece (for the bottom)
- (1) 9-inch piece (for the top)

Screws, 1½ inches and 2 inches

Wood glue

1½-inch brad nails (for nail gun) or finishing nails (for hammer)

Exterior latex enamel paints—yellow, purple, dark red, light green, and dark green

TOOLS

Handsaw or power saw

Electric drill with ¹⁄₁₆-inch and 1¼-inch drill bits

Nail gun or hammer

Pencil

Ruler

Small paintbrush (for detail) and 1-inch paintbrush (for larger areas)

*Note: The actual size of a 1 x 8 is ¾ x 7¼ inches.

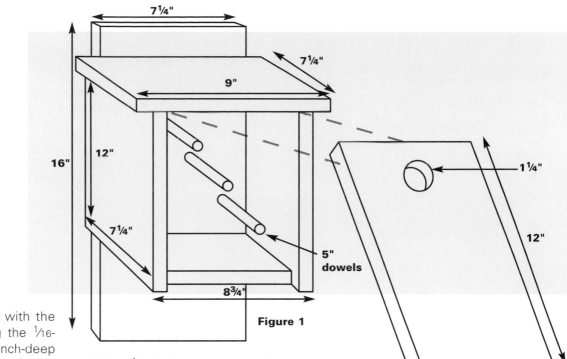

7¼"

7¼"

9"

16"

12"

1¼"

12"

7¼"

5" dowels

8¾"

Figure 1

INSTRUCTIONS

1. Roughen each dowel with the 60-grit sandpaper. Using the ¹⁄₁₆-inch drill bit, drill a 1¼-inch-deep hole into one end of each dowel. Next, drill three ¹⁄₁₆-inch holes, staggered across the back piece so that the holes are not directly over one another. Insert the three 2½-inch screws into these holes through the back, then attach the dowels to the screws.

2. Use wood glue and then nails to assemble the wood pieces. Center the side pieces and attach them to the outer edges of the back. Attach the bottom by sliding it between the sides and against the back, keeping the bottom flush with the ends of the side pieces. Place the top over the sides, flush against the back piece.

3. Drill a 1¼-inch entrance hole through the front piece, positioned 3½ inches below the top edge. (This size will also allow access to nuthatches, titmice, and wrens, but if you want the chickadees to rule the roost, make the entrance hole 1⅛ inches in diameter.)

4. Insert the front between the sides so it is flush with the side pieces. Do not glue; secure with one 1½-inch screw at each side, placed 1½ inches from the top. This construction allows the front door to swing open from the bottom to facilitate cleaning the box.

5. To prepare for painting, sand with 220-grit sandpaper and wipe clean. Lightly sketch the layers of flower petals around the entrance hole; use the ruler for the straight flower stem. Draw the leaves freehand.

6. Use yellow paint for the first layer of petals and let dry. Paint the second layer red and let dry. Then fill in third layer of petals with purple paint and let dry. Fill in the stem with dark green paint and the leaves with light green paint. Add pistils to the yellow petals using the light green paint. Let dry. Then add the dark green lines in the leaves.

7. Paint the top with light green paint. Use the small brush along the edges for a clean line, and then fill in with the 1-inch brush.

HOW TO PERSUADE CHICKADEES TO STAY AROUND

This project will keep resident chickadees toasty and warm through the winter, but you can heighten its appeal by providing plant food sources nearby, as well as potential nesting sites, come spring. You can make sure they have access to seed-heads in winter by growing plants that flower in fall, such as asters, blanket flowers, pincushion flowers, sedum, and salvia. And don't forget that conifers like pine also serve as very important winter food sources. Plants that provide winter or early spring berries include the dogwood, holly, elderberry, cotoneaster, firethorn, rose, and viburnum. Position the roost box on or near a tree that will provide the chickadee with shelter and a place to build its nest. Trees such as oaks or conifers will do nicely.

Wedge Nest Box

This wedge-style birdhouse serves as both a decorative element for the garden and an attractive shelter for violet-green and tree swallows, Carolina wrens, or bluebirds. Customize the birdhouse by choosing paint colors that match your outdoor decor.

MATERIALS

Untreated 1 x 12,* cut as follows:
   (3) 12-inch pieces (for the top,
   front, and sides)
   (1) 18-inch piece
   (for the back)
   (1) 2 x 9 ¾-inch piece
   (for the bottom)

1½-inch galvanized wood screws

Wood glue

2 hinges, 1½ inches

Wood trim, ⅜ x ⅝ inches, at least 50 inches long, cut as follows:
   (2) 12-inch pieces
   (for the top front and
   bottom front)
   (2) 11¼-inch pieces
   (for the top sides)

Finishing nails

Exterior latex paint—two colors of your choice

4 tin tiles, 6 x 6 inches

Exterior-grade adhesive

½-inch carpet tacks

TOOLS

Handsaw or power saw

Pencil

Ruler

Electric drill with 1½-inch bit

Screwdriver

Miter box or power miter saw

Hammer

Small paintbrush

*Note: The actual size of a
1 x 12 is ¾ x 11¼ inches.

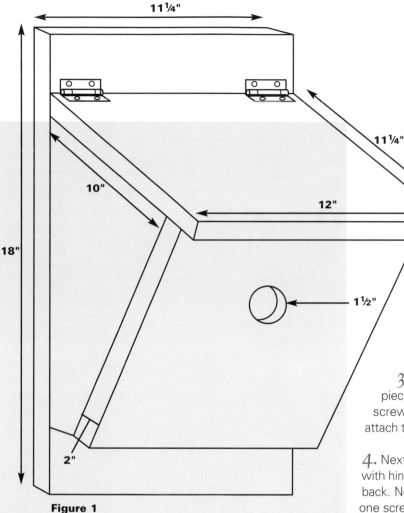

Figure 1

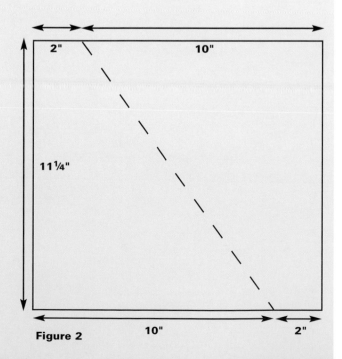

Figure 2

INSTRUCTIONS

I. To make the sides, begin with one of the 11¼ x 12-inch pieces of wood. Measuring from the opposite corners, mark a spot that is 2 inches toward the center of each 12-inch side. Draw a line to connect the marks, and then cut along the line to make the two sides, each measuring 10 inches wide at the top and 2 inches wide at the bottom.

2. On the front piece, drill a 1½-inch hole that is centered and 8 inches up from the bottom edge.

3. Use wood glue and then screws to assemble the wood pieces. First, attach the side pieces onto the back using three screws per side, centering the sides along the back. (Do not attach the sides into the edges of the back.)

4. Next, center the top piece against the back. Secure the top with hinges, attaching them 1 inch from each edge, starting at the back. Now attach the bottom piece to the back and sides, using one screw per side and one screw along the back.

5. Attach the front piece to the sides, using three screws per side, keeping the bottom of the front piece flush with the bottom of the side pieces. This leaves a small gap for ventilation between the top of the front piece and the roof.

6. Use a saw and a miter box or a miter saw at a 45° setting to cut three pieces of trim to fit the front and side edges of the top piece. Cut a piece of trim to fit the bottom edge of the front. Use wood glue and finishing nails to attach the trim.

7. Paint all the surfaces of the nest box in the first color and allow to dry thoroughly. Next, dry brush all the surfaces in the second paint color. (To dry brush, lightly dip the tips of the bristles into the paint, scraping off as much paint as possible. Using little pressure, brush on the surfaces in varying directions.)

8. To finish, arrange the tin tiles on the lid of the box, making sure the lid will open freely. (You can trim them with scissors or tin snips if necessary.) Glue the tiles in place with the exterior-grade adhesive, and place carpet tacks in the corners of each tile.

Screech Owl Box

This elegant nesting box, accented with salvaged materials, is specifically designed for screech owls. Place it in a shady location between 12 to 20 feet above the ground, and wait for the nighttime magic to begin.

MATERIALS

Untreated 1 x 10 board,* cut as follows:
- (1) 22-inch piece (for the back)
- (3) 15-inch pieces
  (for the front and sides)
- (1) 13-inch piece (for the top)
- (1) 7 ¾-inch piece (for the bottom)

Wood glue

1½-inch brad nails (for nail gun)

Finishing nails (for hammer), 1½ inch and ¾ inch

¾-inch quarter-round molding, cut into two 21-inch lengths

Exterior latex paint—white

¾-inch wood trim, salvaged or new, cut as follows:
- (2) 9 ¼-inch pieces
  (for the sides of the top)
- (1) 13-inch piece
  (for the front of the top)

6 x 6-inch wood frame, salvaged or new

Decorative wood scrollwork, salvaged or new

Drawer pull with screw, salvaged or new

Rag

TOOLS

Handsaw or power saw

Nail gun or hammer

Electric drill with 3-inch bit and bit the size of the screw in the drawer pull

Small paintbrush

*Note: The actual size of a 1 x 10 is ¾ x 9 ¼ inches.

INSTRUCTIONS

I. Use wood glue and then nails to assemble the wood pieces. First, attach both sides into the edges of the back, 2½ inches below the top of the back. Next, attach the bottom piece, keeping it flush with the ends of the side pieces.

2. Drill a 3-inch hole in the center of the front, positioned 4 inches below the top. Insert the front between the side pieces, with the front positioned ¼ to ½ inches below the top edge of the sides for ventilation. Do not glue in place; secure with one screw into each side placed 2½ inches below the top. This construction allows the front to swing open from the bottom.

3. Secure the top to the sides, centering it over both sides. Create owl "tufts" by attaching the molding to both sides, the ends of the molding flush with the ends of the sides. Paint the entire box with a coat of whitewash made of 60 percent white paint and 40 percent water. Let dry.

4. Secure the trim in place around the top, beginning with the sides. The longer piece should be on the front.

5. If necessary, drill a three-inch hole in the 6 x 6-inch frame. Secure the frame around the hole, using the 1½-inch finishing nails. Attach the decorative scrollwork using the ¾-inch finishing nails.

6. Drill a hole in the box, placing it in the center of the decorative scrollwork. The hole should be large enough for the screw of the drawer pull. Insert the screw from the inside of the box and attach the drawer pull.

7. Use the paint mixture from step 3 and rub paint on the pieces attached in steps 5 and 6. Wipe off the paint as desired for a weathered effect.

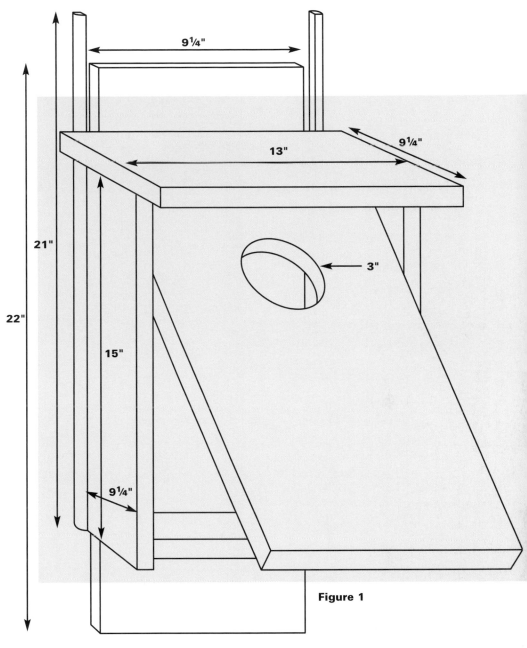

Figure 1

DID YOU KNOW?

Chipping sparrows routinely line their nests with hair, earning them the nickname of "hairbird." Horsehair was their mainstay at one time, but now that horses are no longer a part of everyday life, these birds have become quite resourceful. Even dogs are fair game, as chippings have been known to snatch strands of hair from sleeping canines.

Woodpecker House

The angled edges of this box are somewhat reminiscent of the woodpecker's sharp elongated bill, which is used for drilling into trees. This house is designed to attract the downy woodpecker, a sparrow-sized bird found in both urban and rural areas throughout most of North America.

MATERIALS

Untreated 1 x 6 rough-cut board,* cut as follows:
    (1) 13-inch piece (for top)
    (2) 9-inch pieces (for sides)
    (1) 12-inch piece (for back)
    (1) 4-inch piece (for bottom)
    (1) 7¾-inch piece (for front)

Wood glue

1½-inch brad nails (for nail gun) or finishing nails (for hammer)

220-grit sandpaper

Water-based protective finish—clear gloss

TOOLS

Handsaw or power saw

Nail gun or hammer

Electric drill with 1¼-inch bit

Small paintbrush

*Note: The actual size of a 1 x 6 is ¾ x 5 ½ inches.

INSTRUCTIONS

1. To make the angles in the top piece, measure and mark a point that is 2½ inches down each side. Measure and mark the midpoint of each end, and cut the piece from the midpoint to the marks on each side so that the top comes to a point in the center.

2. To make the angles in the side pieces, trim the top of each piece so it measures 9 inches long in back and 7¾ inches long in front.

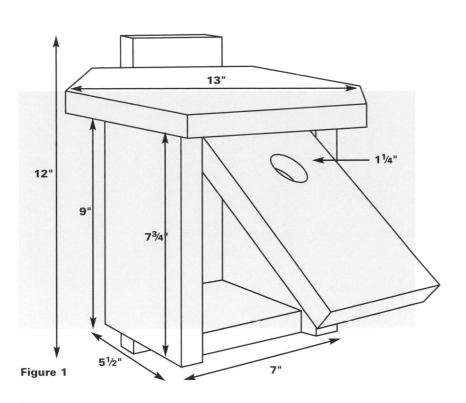

Figure 1

3. Use wood glue and then nails to assemble the pieces. First, attach the sides to the edges of the back, placing them 2 inches below the top edge of the back.

4. Attach the bottom by sliding it between the sides and against the back, keeping the bottom flush with the ends of the side pieces.

5. Drill a 1¼-inch hole in the center of the front piece, about 2 inches below the top. Insert the front piece between the sides; do not glue. Attach with one nail at each side, placed about 1 inch below the top, so the front piece will swing open from the bottom to allow easy access for cleaning the box.

6. Center the top and secure it to the sides, again using wood glue and nails.

7. Sand and wipe clean. Follow the manufacturer's directions to apply the finish; let dry for two hours. Apply a total of three coats of finish.

Tip
A slightly larger entrance hole—1½ inches—will appeal to hairy woodpeckers. Both the downy and the hairy woodpecker will find the box more attractive with several inches of sawdust in the bottom.

DEALING WITH NUISANCE BIRDS

Birds that nest in unexpected places, such as under the eaves of your house, over a doorway, or in the rain gutter, can leave quite a mess. Starlings, house sparrows, and house finches are likely offenders, along with barn swallows and some wren species.

You can caulk, block, or screen off nooks and crannies where they're looking to nest. Another alternative to dealing with house sparrows and starlings is to remove the nest before they set up house. However, with the exception of pigeons, federal and state laws protect all other wild birds—and that includes their nests and eggs. The easiest way to keep these assertive cavity nesters from nesting where they're not wanted is to give them an acceptable alternative: a nest box with an entrance hole designed for their species.

Woodpeckers are known for their characteristic drumming—an annoying habit, especially if they're drumming on your house—but they earn their keep by consuming vast numbers of insects. They're usually attracted to a dead, resonant tree trunk. If they seem to be eyeing your house instead, try one of these techniques: shield the targeted site with hardware cloth or netting hung a few inches away from the wall; make the area less resonant by filling hollow spaces with caulk; or divert their attention with a suet feeder or a nest box carefully placed in a nearby but acceptable location.

Dragonfly Perch

In nature, dragonflies often perch on the sides or tips of stems. Here is a dragonfly perch of copper wire that is whimsical as well as functional.

MATERIALS

6-gauge copper wire, 16 feet
long

18-gauge copper wire, 6 feet
long

2 large, round turquoise beads
(for the eyes)

TOOLS

Wire cutters

Flat-nose pliers

A male blue dasher dragonfly guards his
territory while perching on an aquatic
plant growing near the pond's edge.

Purple martins perch on copper
tubing, which holds a plastic
gourd-style house.

...*fast tracks*

PERCHES

Birds, butterflies, and other winged creatures in search of a place to perch will often alight on garden structures such as trellises, arbors, or pergolas or on smaller, more obscure objects like plant supports, garden stakes, outdoor benches and chairs, or even a wall bracket used for hanging plants. One quick and easy way to expand their perching possibilities is with a simple clothesline or a sturdy wire strung 10 to 12 feet off the ground.

INSTRUCTIONS

I. The dragonfly is made of one continuous piece of 6-gauge wire, beginning with the tail. Straighten about 2½ feet of the wire; at this point, use your hands to start bending the wire, forming the bottom portion of the right wing and then the top portion of the right wing. Form loops for each eye and continue to the left side, this time making the wing from top to bottom. When you've finished creating the wings, twist evenly to form the tail with both ends of the wire. Sink the tail several inches in the ground for stability.

2. Use the pliers to wrap the 18-gauge wire around the middle section where the right and left wings meet. Then pull the wire up through center of this wrapped section and loop it through each eye, adding a turquoise bead before you pull the wire back through the wrapped section. Wrap the wire around the bottom portions of the each wing as necessary and secure it at the center, as shown in the photo below.

Close-up of the dragonfly perch eyes

Orchard Mason Bee Box

If you have fruit trees, berries, or spring-flowering garden plants, the orchard mason bee is an excellent pollinator to have around. In fact, this bee visits over twice as many flowers in a day—1,600 blooms on average—as a honeybee, and effectively pollinates over 90 percent of the flowers it visits.

MATERIALS

Untreated 6 x 6 lumber,* cut to 10½ inches long

Screw eye, 1 inch

Wood and copper-clad postcap

18-gauge copper wire, 8 feet

Finishing nails

TOOLS

Power saw

Ruler

Pencil

Electric drill with ⁵⁄₁₆-inch bit (brad-point bit optional)

Wire cutters

Hammer

*Note: The actual size of a 6 x 6 is 5½ x 5½ inches.

INSTRUCTIONS

1. To create nesting holes for the orchard mason bee, drill a series of 5/16-inch holes, spaced roughly 1 inch apart, all on one face of the block. Mason bees will nest in holes from 3 to 8 inches deep that are open on one end only; when drilling holes, never drill completely through, stopping short about ½ inch from the back of the block.

2. To re-create this layout, mark 9 rows of 5 holes each, for a total of 45 holes. Measure the exact depth of the block, as shrinkage and planing can cause your lumber to have slightly different dimensions than is specified here. Mark your drill bit at the spot that is ½ inch less than the block's depth to keep from drilling all the way through, then drill a 5/16-inch hole at every pencil mark. (A brad-point bit will leave a smoother hole.)

3. To hang, fasten a screw eye in the top center of the block. Pierce or drill a small hole in the wood-and-copper postcap. Cut an 8-foot length of copper wire and fold it in half. Slip the wire onto the screw eye. Thread the wire ends through the hole in the postcap and slide the postcap into place on the block. Nail the postcap in place with the finishing nails. Use the free ends of the wire to hang your bee box.

Figure 1

10½"

5½"   5½"

Tip
The orchard mason bee lays its eggs in the spring, so be sure to set out the empty bee box by February. A protected location facing southeast is best. Their forage range is about 200 feet, so situate the box within that distance of the plants you want the bees to pollinate. Attach the box under the eaves or on the side of a building to keep the bee box from swaying in the wind. Keep in mind that most pesticides are toxic to bees, so do avoid their use.

Once all the holes are vacated, you'll need to clean the bee nest box as soon as possible to prevent disease. In the spring, once females leave the nest box, they immediately mate and start laying yet another batch of eggs, so you might only have a week or two when the box is empty. You can soak wooden bee blocks in a weak chlorine solution at a ratio of 1 part bleach to 10 parts water or sterilize them in a warm oven set at about 200°F (93.3°C).

Orchard mason bee

THE ORCHARD MASON BEE

The orchard mason bee *(Osmia lignaria)*, also known as the blue orchard bee, is so gentle that it never stings unless harshly handled. Slightly smaller than a honeybee, the shiny blue-black bee is a solitary nester, laying her eggs in a hole not much bigger than her body.

Typically, orchard mason bees nest in any natural cavity measuring from ¼ to 5/16 inches in diameter, such as holes left by tree borers or woodpeckers. In the spring, females form a mound in each hole made of pollen and nectar that provides the larvae with food. She then deposits one egg and uses mud to construct a chamber. Continuing this process until the hole is filled, she then seals the entrance with a wall of mud. With the following spring's arrival, usually from mid-March through May, the previous season's brood, which went into hibernation the previous fall as winged adults, emerges from their overwintering cocoons and adobe mud cells.

Orchard Mason Bee
Nesting Pipe

The natural nesting holes needed by orchard mason bees are often in short supply. This colorful nesting pipe provides just the right kind of holes these beneficial, nonaggressive bees seek.

MATERIALS

Piece of schedule 40 PVC pipe, 3 inches in diameter and 8½ inches long

Schedule 40 PVC cap, 3 inches in diameter

Exterior latex enamel spray paint—butterscotch

Exterior high-gloss latex enamel paint—blue

PVC adhesive

2 screw eyes, 1 inch long

Piece of wire or cord, length of your choice

100 plastic or paper straws, 7½ inches long and ¼ to 5⁄16 inch in diameter

TOOLS

Power saw

Small paintbrush

Electric drill with bit

INSTRUCTIONS

1. Cut one end of the PVC pipe at an angle to create a roof overhang. When finished, the top of the pipe should measure 8½ inches, and the bottom should measure 7½ inches.

2. Paint both the pipe and the cap with the butterscotch spray paint, spraying partway inside the pipe; let dry. Paint the rim of the cap with the contrasting blue paint; let dry. Attach the cap to the flat end of the pipe using the PVC adhesive; let dry.

3. Drill two pilot holes on top, one in the cap and one on the opposite end. Insert the screw eyes, then thread with wire or cord to hang. Bundle the straws and insert into the pipe.

4. Hang the nesting pipe in an area protected from wind, with the opening facing any direction between south and east to catch the morning sun. Always be sure to select a pesticide-free area when choosing the location of your project.

Tip

The nesting pipe is adaptable to any length of straw. Simply start with PVC pipe that is one inch longer than your straws. You can also alter the length of the straws if necessary by cutting them to size or folding them in half. Keeping the nesting pipe clean is easy: simply remove the straws and replace them with a fresh supply. To learn a little more about the orchard mason bee, see The Orchard Mason Bee on page 109.

Chapter 7

ADDING WATER

American goldfinch at birdbath

A bubbling fountain sits in the midst of colorful flowers, palms, container plants, and other perennials in a tropical courtyard garden.

It's quite amusing to watch birds in a backyard pond or birdbath. They quickly dunk their heads into a shallow pool of water and splash their wings to soak their backs. It's especially fun when several birds bathe together. Goldfinches often perform this ritual in a birdbath located in our kitchen garden, with me watching from a bench just three feet away! They don't seem to mind my being there as long as I don't make any sudden movements.

Even a simple water source, such as this natural depression in a rock, can provide a refreshing place for birds, butterflies, and beneficial insects to bathe and drink.

Simple Water SOURCES

Simple water sources—from the obvious to the obscure—can quench the thirst of a number of backyard creatures. Many birds will use a shallow, water-filled saucer or a clean garbage can lid turned upside down. Mourning doves seem to especially appreciate the occasional water-filled saucer that's placed on the ground underneath our oak tree. We find that placing rocks or stones in one side of the saucer makes for a bird-friendly water source that doubles as a butterfly drinking station. You just need to be sure the tops of the rocks or stones are slightly above water level so they provide suitable places where butterflies can perch.

You can also use a hose to wet the foliage of trees and shrubs for smaller birds like warblers and hummingbirds that like to "leaf bathe." Water that collects on concave surfaces of trees, shrubs, and plants—like dogwood, spicebush, holly, or even hostas—form minuscule pools of water that are the perfect-sized bath for small birds. Sprinklers used to water lawns or garden beds offer another water source for hummingbirds. Actually, they bathe on the wing as they buzz back and forth through the fine spray, which is always great fun to watch. Even soaker hoses placed in garden beds attract butterflies, dragonflies, and other beneficial insects.

Spray hostas with your hose, and you've created an instant leaf bath for smaller birds like warblers and hummingbirds.

Birdbath BASICS

Birdbaths are easy to install in your wildlife garden. In addition to meeting wildlife needs, they essentially function as garden sculptures that reflect your individual sense of style. Whether the design reflects Old World charm or that of a casual cottage, or whether it reveals inspirations from Asia or a sense of whimsy, bird-baths do it all with sensible style.

Most songbirds feel safest with shallow water and solid footing, so sturdy baths that gently slope to a center depth of no more than 3 inches are best. If the surface of your birdbath is smooth, you can rough it up with sandpaper before fill-ing it with water or apply safety footing, like the decals sold for bathtubs. Deeper baths can be made more bird-friendly by placing a few partially submerged rocks or branches to serve as perching platforms. Fill the bath with large pebbles or river stones to create pools of shallow water, and you may discover hummingbirds and butterflies adopting the bath as their own.

Any shallow receptacle can be used as a birdbath—homemade, ready-made, or otherwise. For example, you can simply set a waterproof bowl or large plant saucer on a flat rock or log stump. Or you can sink any kind of basin into the

Iris and lupines take center stage in a small bog garden located near a backyard pond.

New Zealand hair sedge surrounds a simple fountain: an urn turned on its side that spills water into a basin.

A concrete birdbath is even more enticing when set in the middle of groundcovers. But why not add something extra, such as this statue of a girl, placed on or near the bath?

ground, place it at ground level surrounded by a border of low-growing plants, or use rocks, bark, or thick branches to hold the bath in place and help it blend in with the landscape. If you'd like, let your imagination run wild and create a birdbath from found materials or recycled objects. For example, mount a ceramic or terra-cotta saucer on drainage tile and decorate with mosaic tiles collected from chipped dishes.

But if you're not feeling especially creative, ready-made birdbaths are the convenient way to go. They come in so many sizes and materials that they're as much fun to shop for as they are for birds to use. You can purchase baths that you set on the ground or on a companion pedestal or baths that hang from a rope or chain. Sizes vary from smaller basins sized for single-occupant use to basins with a diameter of 20 inches or more, roomy enough to accommodate a bevy of birds.

You can also turn recycled objects into a birdbath. Here, a recycled boat hatch becomes a birdbath, complete with a perching rock.

A monk birdbath—surrounded by marigolds, hummingbird mint, and alliums—becomes the focal point in a garden filled with flowering perennials, herbs, and fruit trees.

Ready-made birdbaths are available in a variety of styles and materials. Here, a glazed terra-cotta birdbath brings added elegance to a bed of flowering azaleas and hyacinths.

Ready-made birdbaths come in plastic, synthetic stone or concrete, terra cotta or glazed ceramics, and natural materials. While plastic baths are typically the least expensive, they are also often the least attractive. In addition, they have smooth surfaces that don't provide enough of a foothold for birds and may not be as sturdy as other types of birdbaths. While convincingly mimicking the look of the real thing, synthetic stone or concrete birdbaths have the advantage of being lightweight. Baths made of terra cotta or glazed ceramics come in a wide range of colors and designs, yet may not be the best choice for winter use as they sometimes crack during hard freezes. By far, the most aesthetically appealing—at least in my eyes—are those fashioned from natural materials. You can opt for a handcrafted bath made of copper, aluminum, cast iron, or other metal, or choose from baths made of cement, concrete, or natural stone.

With a nearby cover of grapevines, finches flock to a birdbath set in our large garden.

SETTING UP THE BIRDBATH

The best location for a birdbath varies, depending on the vegetation, potential predators, and the bird species most likely to visit your garden. Some birds prefer a bath underneath the protective shelter of a tree or brushy cover, especially if hawks are in the area. And yet most songbirds prefer a water source that's located in a sunny, open area within 10 to 20 feet of shelter. That way they have time to make a quick escape to nearby cover if they spot a neighborhood cat or other predator. The branches also double as perches where they can preen to their heart's content after bathing.

A single birdbath is a welcome addition in any wildlife garden. Even better are multiple birdbaths, guaranteed to attract a variety of birds to your yard. You can place baths in different locations and at varying heights—even hang one from a tree. In our own garden, we placed one bath at ground level under a tree and another about 2 feet high in a garden bed right next to a tree. There's an elevated bath in a semiclearing about five feet from shelter and a large pedestal bath on the courtyard patio by a bed that's 15 feet away from cover. When choosing where to place a birdbath, don't just take the birds' needs into account. Make sure you pick a convenient spot, so you can fill and clean the bath with ease. And you want to have a good view of the birds as they drink and splash in the water.

TAKING CARE

It almost goes without saying that a birdbath is just an empty bowl unless you keep it filled with water. How often a bath needs replenishing can vary—from every day to once a week, depending on its location and size as well as the weather conditions. For example, water in a small birdbath can quickly evaporate during hot summer days. Algae, feathers, bird droppings, and garden litter dirty the water, and dirty water can spread disease. So it's equally important to be sure the water is clean by changing it frequently and by periodically cleaning the basin.

Also remember that birds need water in winter as well as in the warmer months. You can continue supplying water even during the coldest weather by adding a submersible, thermostatically controlled water heater specifically designed for outdoor birdbaths. They are generally sold at garden and home improvement centers as well as farm stores and bird supply stores. The heater will keep the water from freezing so resident songbirds can enjoy fresh water at any time.

DID YOU KNOW?

Practice does make perfect, at least it does in nature. Researchers have discovered that while a zebra finch may practice singing thousands of times while awake, it also mentally rehearses the song during sleep until it can sing the song with perfection, which in the case of a zebra finch usually takes about two months.

MATERIALS

Clay or pottery saucer (a salvaged birdbath basin also works well), 16 inches in diameter

Smooth pebbles to fill saucer

Water

Beneficial Bug Bath

It's not just birds that need water, you know. Insects also need it to survive, and this bath for beneficial bugs offers a perfect oasis. Locate it on the ground, a large rock, a tree stump, or an upside-down container.

INSTRUCTIONS

I. Decide where to place your bug bath. Pollen- and nectar-producing plants—like sunflowers, lavender, purple coneflower, and sweet alyssum—attract beneficial bugs, so the insects are likely to find the bath faster if you place it near or in a garden bed.

2. Now create a safe place for the beneficial bugs to drink; most insects will drown in a saucer filled only with water unless you provide drinking perches. After you've chosen the location for your bath, fill the saucer with pebbles or use them to create a series of steps or islands where insects can land and drink without danger. (You can also use lava rocks for visual interest.)

3. Fill the saucer with water to within ¼ inch of the rim. Refresh the saucer with water when needed. Keep in mind that water can quickly evaporate during the hot, dry days of summer and may need to be refilled daily.

Flowerpot Birdbath

You don't need elaborate structures to make your yard a haven for wildlife. All you need are three carefully chosen flowerpots, a plant saucer, and some epoxy to create this delightful birdbath.

MATERIALS

3 clay pots, 8 inches in diameter

Epoxy

Clay saucer, 12 inches in diameter

INSTRUCTIONS

I. Select your flowerpots carefully. For this project, you need pots that don't stack tightly together, as shown in the photograph. If you're purchasing new flowerpots, test them at the store before you buy them.

2. To create the pedestal, place the first pot upside down on the ground. Then add a line of epoxy around the base of the pot. Place the second pot on top of the first, upside down. Add epoxy as on the first pot, and then place the remaining pot on top, also upside down.

3. To finish the birdbath, use the epoxy to attach the bottom of the clay saucer to the flowerpot pedestal. When all is dry, carefully move the birdbath to its location in your yard. Fill with water.

Hanging Bamboo Birdbath

Here's a simple project that's certain to attract winged visitors. Because it's lightweight and portable, you can locate it virtually anywhere in your yard.

MATERIALS

4 bamboo stakes,
each ½ x 20 inches

4 wood screws, 1 inch long

Plastic plant saucer,
14 inches in diameter

20 feet of jute

Epoxy

Nontoxic glue, such as white craft glue

10 feet of chain, ¼ inch in diameter

4 binder rings, 2 inches in diameter

Key ring, 1 inch in diameter

1 S-hook

TOOLS

Measuring tape

Pencil

Handsaw

Drill with small drill bit

Screwdriver

Scissors

Pliers

INSTRUCTIONS

1. If you need to cut the bamboo to size, measure and cut it with the handsaw. You need four stakes that are each 20 inches long.

2. Arrange the pieces of bamboo so they form a square frame on which the saucer will sit; you'll have overlap at the ends. (Be sure the saucer fits on top of, and not in, the bamboo frame.) The bamboo pieces should be at right angles to one another.

3. Drill a pilot hole in each of the corners where the pieces overlap, and then screw the pieces together. Check to ensure the bamboo frame is square and the saucer fits. You can straighten the piece now if necessary.

4. Cut four pieces of jute that are each 5 feet long. Wrap one end of the jute around each corner and knot, leaving a tail that will later be used to tie to the other end. Wrap the jute around the two pieces of bamboo, alternating directions. Be sure to hide the head of the screw. When you've wrapped all the jute, knot it with the tail.

5. Glue the bottom of the saucer to the bamboo on each of the four sides, using just a dab of epoxy. Place a small dab of nontoxic glue on each knot of the jute and let dry.

6. Separate the chain into two pieces that are each 5 feet long by using the pliers to open a link in the middle.

7. On each end of the pieces of chain, attach a binder ring. Place the binder rings around the overlapped corner of the bamboo frame. Close the binder rings and secure each with a dab of epoxy, if desired.

8. Run the key ring through the center link of each length of chain. Loop the S-hook through the key ring to hang the birdbath.

Eight-spotted skimmer dragonfly

DID YOU KNOW?

Even though we usually picture dragonflies in flight, they actually live much of their lives as aquatic creatures. Females generally deposit eggs on or near water—directly on the water's surface, into mud at the water's edge, in the tissues of wetland vegetation, or in wet, rotting wood. Known as naiads or nymphs, the chunky larvae live anywhere from a few weeks to approximately five years; adults, in contrast, don't live for more than a month or two. During their larval stage, dragonflies live almost exclusively in fresh water and breathe through gills located inside the tip of the abdomen.

Making a Miniature Wetland

If you're willing to provide water on a larger scale, consider creating your own miniature wetland. Since it provides an ideal environment for moisture-loving plants—from grasses and ferns to flowering perennials, shrubs, and trees—a wetland serves as a valuable source of food, shelter, and nesting sites for wildlife. Many species of iris, sedges, and other plants attractive to butterflies and hummingbirds—like cardinal flower, swamp milkweed, and Joe-pye weed—thrive in a wetland garden's damp soil. Some species of dragonflies and damselflies frequent boggy areas to mate, to feed on insects, and to perch on vegetation.

MATERIALS

Coarse sand or gravel*

Flexible pond liner**

Loam***

Edging materials, such as stone or brick

TOOLS

Garden hose, heavy rope, or powdered limestone for marking bog site

Shovel and pick

Measuring tape

Rake

Sharp scissors or utility knife for cutting the liner

*You'll need to calculate how many cubic feet of sand or gravel you'll require. First convert the bog's dimensions to inches by multiplying by 12. Calculate the volume by multiplying the width x length x the desired depth of sand or gravel (usually 1 or 2 inches) and then divide by 1728 (the number of cubic inches in a cubic foot), and you'll get the number of cubic feet required. For example, to fill a 4 x 3-foot bog with 2 inches of sand or gravel, you will need 2 cubic feet of sand or gravel (the product of 48 x 36 x 2 divided by 1728). If you get a fraction of a cubic foot, round it up.

**To calculate the size of the liner you need, measure the bog's maximum width and length, then add to each dimension 2 times the maximum depth plus 2 feet. For example a 4 x 3 x 2-foot bog would require a 10 x 9-foot liner (4+4+2=10 feet; 3+4+2=9 feet).

***Two parts each garden soil, compost, and peat moss plus one part sand or vermiculite.

Figure 1

Liner

Loam

Sand and gravel

122

A naturally damp area creates an ideal site for a small bog garden. This example includes moisture-loving plants like ferns, hostas, and various ground covers.

INSTRUCTIONS

Few backyards have the space for the kinds of large wetlands found in nature. However, you can create a backyard-friendly, small-scale bog that will function in much the same way. You may already have a prime location for such a wetland garden. It could be a soggy spot that drains poorly, a depression in the landscape that holds water, or any other damp area in your yard. The site may have standing water year-round or only during the rainy season.

Even if your yard lacks a low-lying area or wet spot, you (and the wildlife) can still enjoy the benefits of a wetland garden by constructing one yourself. The goal is to create an area that retains moisture without being completely watertight.

1. Choose an open, level site that receives at least five hours of sun a day. Use the garden hose, rope, or powdered limestone to mark the outline of your bog on the ground. Dig a hole with gradually sloping sides to a maximum depth that can range from 1½ to 3 feet.

2. Remove any protruding roots or rocks from the site. Cover the bottom of the excavated area with a 2-inch layer of damp sand to protect the liner from potential punctures.

3. Next you'll need to line the hole with heavy plastic or a flexible, heavy-duty polyethylene pond liner. Unfold the pond liner loosely over the hole, leaving an even overlap on all sides. (The liner is easier to work with if you install it on a warm, sunny day.) Smooth the liner into position.

4. Since the area needs to be water-retentive, not watertight, use the sharp scissors or utility knife to puncture the liner around the side about halfway up from the bottom. Puncture holes 12 inches apart for a smaller bog or up to 3 feet apart for a larger bog. However, you may want to leave the liner intact if the annual rainfall in your area is minimal. Leave an overlap of 6 to 12 inches, depending on the size of the bog, and then trim off the excess.

5. Once the liner is in place, cover the bottom with a 1- to 2-inch layer of coarse sand or gravel. Next, fill the hole with a nice loam that retains moisture. You can follow the directions on page 122 for a good all-purpose loam, or you can make the mix mostly peat-based if you'll be growing true bog plants like bog orchids, sundews, or pitcher plants that require acidic soil.

6. Place rocks or stones around the wetland's edge to cover the overlap and secure the liner in place. Edging the wetland with natural materials provides a visual transition that helps blend it in with the surroundings.

Cattails

Lysimachia

PLANTS FOR YOUR BOG GARDEN

Your climate will determine which plants you can grow. If you live in an area with enough rainfall so that the soil is always saturated, you'll have more plant options than if you live in an area that experiences alternating wet and dry periods. However, plants like lysimachia, cattails, houttuynia, and New England asters usually do fine with fluctuating moisture levels as long as the soil doesn't dry up completely for an extended period of time. And even though horsetail is classified as a plant that consistently needs moist soil or shallow water, our native horsetail flourishes each year in a partially shaded area that dries out in the summer.

If you want your wetland plants to flourish and attract winged wildlife, keep the soil moist to slightly moist at all times. A densely planted wetland works best since it allows less evaporation than one with areas of exposed soil surface. And a mulch of compost or leaves will help retain moisture and shade the surface until the plants fill in. When moisture does evaporate, water your wetland garden. Be especially vigilant during periods of hot, dry weather.

Start with this list of wetland recommendations, and then check with your local nursery or garden center to find out which might work best for your situation.

PLANTS FOR SHADY, MOIST, OR WET SOIL

Golden sedge
(*Carex elata* 'Aurea')

Moor grass (*Molinia* spp.)

Lady fern and Japanese painted fern (*Athyrium* spp*.)

Royal fern and cinnamon fern (*Osmunda* spp.)

Chain ferns (*Woodwardia* spp.)

Creeping Jenny (*Lysimachia nummularia*)

Gunnera (*Gunnera* spp.)

Hostas (*Hosta* spp.)

Chameleon plant (*Houttuynia cordata*)

Jack-in-the-pulpit (*Arisaema triphyllum*)

Marsh betony (*Stachys palustris*)

Marsh marigold (*Caltha palustris*)

Meadowsweet (*Filipendula* spp.)

Spiderwort (*Tradescantia virginiana*)

Scarlet monkeyflower (*Mimulus cardinalis*)

Turtlehead (*Chelone lyonii*)

PLANTS FOR SUNNY, MOIST, OR WET SOIL

Cattails (*Typha* spp.)

Common calla (*Zantedeschia aethiopica*)

Horsetail (*Equisetum* spp.)

Iris—yellow flag, blue flag, Japanese, Siberian, Louisiana (*Iris* spp.)

Rush (*Juncus*)

Sweet flag (*Acorus* spp.)

Switch grass (*Panicum virgatum*)

Water plantain (*Alisma plantago-aquatica*)

Astilbe (*Astilbe arendsii*)

Bog arum (*Calla palustris*)

Cardinal flower (*Lobelia cardinalis*)

Hardy canna (*Thalia dealbata*)

Joe-Pye weed (*Eupatorium purpureum*)

New England aster (*Aster novae-angliae*)

Swamp milkweed (*Asclepias incarnata*)

Water hibiscus (*Hibiscus moscheutos palustris*)

Water parsnip (*Sium Suave*)

TREES & SHRUBS FOR WET SOIL

Ash (*Fraxinus* spp.)

River birch (*Betula nigra*)

Box elder (*Acer negundo*)

Red maple (*Acer rubrum*)

Pawpaw (*Asimina triloba*)

Hawthorns (*Crataegus* spp.)

Swamp white oak (*Quercus bicolor*)

Willows (*Salix* spp.)

Red osier dogwood (*Cornus stolonifera*)

Winterberry (*Ilex verticillata*)

Spicebush (*Lindera benzoin*)

* *Spp.* is the abbreviation for the plural of *species*.

Japanese iris and astilbe

PUDDLING SITES AND THE SOUND OF WATER

Mud puddles and the sound of water: did you know how alluring they are to butterflies, birds, and other winged wildlife?

Mud puddles don't just attract mischievous children. They make a contribution to butterfly reproduction because the nutrients male butterflies acquire from puddles strengthen their sperm. Much like the highly concentrated nutrients in dried fruit (as compared with fresh), they become even more concentrated once the water evaporates. Consequently, butterflies often continue visiting these puddling sites until they're nearly dry.

You can create an artificial puddle by burying a washbasin or large shallow pan filled with a mix of wet sand and soil. Place a few sticks or rocks on the surface to create places for them to perch, and be sure to fill the bucket with water as needed to keep the puddle moist. For added convenience, locate the portable puddle underneath a leaky faucet or hose, or place it in a sunny area near the spray from a sprinkler or fountain.

And just the sound of water—regardless of whether it's gurgling or simply dripping—can make a dramatic difference between a run-of-the-mill resting spot frequented by a few birds or an exceptional habitat winged creatures find irresistibly appealing. One of the simplest ways to attract birds with sound is to place a dripper over a birdbath. Bird supply stores and garden centers offer a variety of drippers and dripper systems. Or you can make your own by hanging a bucket, old watering can, or gallon-sized plastic milk jug a few feet above your birdbath. Drill or puncture a small hole at the lower edge of the container and fill with water. The hole should be small enough so the water drips out slowly—about 10 to 20 drips a minute. That way you won't have to fill the container quite as often.

You can transform a shallow bowl into a deluxe birdbath by placing it on a rock and adding a dripper. Here, a birdbath with dripper is set among such bird-attracting plants as penstemon, globe amaranth, ornamental grasses, and shrubs.

125

Chapter 8

ENJOYING THE SHOW

Once you've gone to the trouble to attract birds, butterflies, and other winged wonders to your yard, make sure you take the time to enjoy the show. As with any outing, a little preparation will make the experience much more enjoyable. Filling the feeder and watching the frenzied activity that follows is always fun, but it's especially rewarding when you can identify exactly which birds have come to call. Knowing the spots where butterflies are most likely to remain still long enough for you to see them up close will give your wildlife watching an exciting new dimension. And you can extend your wildlife watching pleasure into the evening hours when you discover which nectar flowers attract moths.

A white peacock butterfly lingers on an aster flower while nectaring.

Laying the GROUNDWORK

At any time of the day from early spring to late autumn, you can usually find some type of winged wildlife in action. As you'll soon learn, the best time to watch for butterflies, for instance, isn't always the best time to enjoy birds or moths. Likewise the wildlife species you're most likely to observe vary with the season. Educating yourself about when and where you have the best chances of observing wildlife in action, as well as how to identify and interact with winged creatures, can dramatically enhance your viewing experience many times over. Of course, a little bit of patience and a few basic tools always help. If you've carefully laid the groundwork for great viewing, you'll find surprises around every corner.

Sometimes if you manage to stay very still, you'll be rewarded with the pleasure of watching a dark-eyed junco scratching its way across the ground.

Purple chairs nestled against a blue lattice backdrop provide the ideal vantage point for this backyard habitat filled with wildlife-friendly plants like conifers, hostas, ornamental grasses, and heavenly bamboo. A grass path is accented by the lavender-blue of flowering catmint.

BIRD WATCHING

During the spring, the season's first songbirds and hummingbirds arrive, courtship and mating rituals take place, and nest boxes are filled to capacity. In our own yard in western Oregon, for example, swallows arrive each spring to inhabit most of our 30 nest boxes. In summer, we watch parents feeding their young and fledglings leaving the nest. It's also the best time to catch a glimpse of colorful birds, such as hummingbirds, orioles, and tanagers. With the fall, new species of birds pass through as they migrate, and even dur-

ing the winter, we're treated to flocks of resident birds at the feeder.

For the most part, birds are creatures of habit, generally feeding, bathing, and preening at the same time each day; of course, they use the sun rather than a clock to schedule their activities. Since birds busy themselves in a flurry of activity during the early morning hours, this is often your best opportunity to listen to their calls or songs and watch them feed. The number of birds I see while harvesting produce on an early summer morning

never ceases to amaze me. It's the time when I can count on watching robins searching for worms, swallows feeding their nestlings, nuthatches climbing headfirst down trees, and flocks of goldfinches either perching on the fence or taking turns hopping from bed to bed.

Bird-watching in the afternoon has its own charms. While you may see a bird only here and there, the ones you do see are often more relaxed. This can lead to greater opportunities for close observation and one-on-one interaction. There have been times when I've sat in one spot for an extended period while hand-pulling weeds and a dark-eyed junco scratched its way across the ground to within a foot of my hand. Often a black-capped chickadee or song sparrow will fly over and then perch on the arm of the bench where I'm quietly sitting. And the afternoon is when you're most likely to be able to watch birds at the bath.

Asters make this a favorite nectaring spot for a giant swallowtail butterfly.

An elegant sphinx moth hovers at dusk to dine on verbena flowers.

BUTTERFLY VIEWING

Summer and sun offer the optimal conditions for viewing butterflies. Cold-blooded creatures, butterflies won't even begin to flutter until the temperature reaches at least 60°F (15.6°C); they're most active when the temperature is 80°F (26.7°C) or more. Because butterflies can't fly without the benefit of the sun's heat, they often take shelter during cool or cloudy weather. Discovering their hiding spots can be fun. Good places to look include trees or shrubs, an open shed, loosely stacked brush piles, or beneath fallen bark or leaves.

And then there are the times when butterflies become so focused—usually when they're feeding on nectar or basking in the sun—that they remain almost motionless with their wings spread open for moments at a time. Such moments allow you to see every detail— from the wings' intense colors to their complex patterns. Butterflies startle more easily than birds, so it's best to position yourself next to a regular basking site, a fruit-feeding station, or a bed of nectar-rich flowers. If you're lucky, a butterfly may even land on your shoulder.

A voracious predator, this Western pondhawk dragonfly may look innocent enough, but this species has been known to snatch dragonflies their own size.

DID YOU KNOW?

If you've ever been out in the sun on a warm day wearing dark-colored clothing, you know how quickly your body heats up. Most butterflies bask in the sun with wings outstretched to absorb solar heat. When sulphur butterflies bask, however, they do so with their wings closed and turned sideways to the sun, a practice referred to as lateral basking. The dark scales underneath their wings help their bodies absorb heat more rapidly in much the same way your dark clothing does.

OTHER WINGED WONDERS

Although most moths are nocturnal, there are day-flying moths, such as some species of tiger and sphinx moths. The best way to observe such day-flying moths is to be on the lookout for them in your flower garden any time from late morning to dusk when they're likely to be feeding or drinking. At night, you need look no further than your porch light if you want to observe these winged creatures. Moths will fly toward a bright light and often circle or spiral around it, although no one really understands why. One hypothesis is that the moths are not really attracted to artificial lights. What's actually happening is their navigational systems, thought to reckon by the moon, are thrown out of kilter by the brilliance of a light bulb.

Seen here on a zinnia flower, the colorfully striped hover fly (syrphid) is an effective pollinator, plus it doesn't bite or sting.

Carnivorous dragonflies and damselflies find their meals on or near water, where they also breed. So wetlands, such as backyard ponds, are the best places to observe these ravenous creatures, although you might also find them in your garden perched on stems, grasses, sticks, or twigs. Like butterflies, most dragonflies and damselflies need a minimum temperature to fly, in the neighborhood of 50°F (10°C) for most species. Many species generate heat internally by shivering or rapidly beating their wings. Some dragonflies raise their body temperature by basking in sunny locations—either perched on a flower or stem, on floating vegetation, on bare sunny paths, or on rocks or stones.

You can attract beneficial insects—like the lady beetle, lacewing, syrphid (or hover fly), and praying mantis—by growing the pollen and nectar flowers that meet their needs for protein and energizing carbohydrates. Another way to make your yard a hospitable place for these beneficials is by providing shelter in the form of grasses, ground covers, garden cover crops, and shrubs or hedgerows. Brush piles, leaf litter, and garden mulch all offer protection as well. A safe place to drink is yet another necessity. You'll be rewarded with both a chance to watch these creatures in action and with the eventual appearance of larvae that consume hordes of pests.

A white-crowned sparrow at one of the feeders in our courtyard garden

A Steller's jay, easily identified by its all-black head and crest, at the same courtyard garden feeder

Uncovering *the* CLUES

Birds, butterflies, moths, and dragonflies have certain characteristics that make each species unique. Knowing how to look for those characteristics will give you an added advantage when trying to identify the winged wildlife you find in your garden.

IDENTIFYING BIRDS

Being able to identify birds by sight is all about paying attention to details. When trying to distinguish one species from another, always begin by noting any obvious characteristics, starting with size. Is the bird the size of a sparrow, a robin, or a jay? What colors do you see, and where do you see them? Make a note of the bird's field marks, the characteristic colors, patterns, or structures that help in identifying species. For example, look at a bird's chest to see whether it's plain, spotted, or streaked. The shape of the head, wings, and tail as well as the shape of a bird's bill are visual clues as well. For example, brown creepers and wrens typically have long, slightly curved bills whereas chickadees' bills are short and stout. With their strong, thick bills, evening grosbeaks are especially easy to spot.

Identifying a bird by its call certainly takes a bit of practice, as well as something of a skillful ear. A given bird's vocabulary can vary from a relatively short, simple call—chirps, warbles, squawks, peeps, and cheeps—to a complex, extended melody. And that melody can take on a slightly different tone, depending on the bird's age and sex as well as its regional dialect and the time of the year.

Some bird vocalizations are unmistakable—once you hear them, you'll never forget them. A good example is the red-tailed hawk, with its resounding, high-pitched cry that stirs the soul. But the key to identifying a bird by sound is to be able to hear how the bird actually sounds. After all, reading descriptions of a bird's cry in a guide can't compare with hearing the actual call or song. (What exactly does *keeeer* sound like, anyway?) Fortunately, there's a variety of audio field guides that make birding by ear easier than ever. You can buy backyard and regionally specific bird song recordings on CD and tape. There's even a complete, palm-sized portable unit you can take with you anywhere, even if you're only going as far as your backyard.

CARBON COPIES

Just when you think you've got a certain bird's call or song down pat, along comes the mimic—a bird that copies the sounds made by other birds. Actually, it's believed that about 20 percent of perching birds imitate other birds' calls and cries. For example, a starling can imitate the sound of a killdeer or nighthawk, and both scrub jays and blue jays perform their slightly less resonant versions of a red-tailed hawk's cry. The northern mockingbird is perhaps the best-known mimic of the passerines (birds that typically have feet adapted for perching) and is reputed to mimic more than just birdcalls. The sounds of squirrels, frogs, crickets, and even a rusty gate are all thought to be part of this bird's repertoire.

A solitary pine white butterfly at rest on a pincushion flower

SPOTTING BUTTERFLIES, MOTHS, & DRAGONFLIES

Identifying butterflies, moths, and dragonflies is much like identifying birds: it's all about paying attention to details, such as colors, patterns, and size, as well as the time of year the insect is active.

Butterflies and moths do have their differences, and knowing them is handy since there are moths that fly by day. The most obvious way to distinguish butterflies from moths at a glance is by the way in which they hold their wings when at rest. Most butterflies hold their wings together and upright over their backs while moths generally hold their wings flat or like a tent over their furry, stout bodies. Also, butterflies have slender antennae that end in a swollen tip. Moth antennae, in contrast, are feathery or threadlike and lack the butterflies' swollen tips.

Dragonflies and damselflies both belong to an order of insects called Odonata. Although similar to each other, damselflies are more delicate, slender, and smaller than dragonflies and tend to have a weaker, more fluttery flight pattern. As with butterflies and moths, the easiest way to tell them apart is to observe what they do with their wings when at rest: damselflies fold their wings either partially or completely against their bodies, while dragonflies hold theirs outstretched. The eyes also provide another important clue. Damselflies have eyes that bulge to the side rather than across their heads, as dragonfly eyes do. When trying to distinguish particular species, look at their overall size and style of flight. Also check out the color and pattern on the abdomen and thorax, the color of the eyes and face, the shape and position of the wings, and the way in which they perch—which can be vertically, horizontally, or diagonally.

Gearing UP

When it comes to wildlife viewing, as with any activity, a few ground rules and some essential tools always make for a more enjoyable and productive experience. For starters, make sure to include one or two places to sit when you design your wildlife garden—a cozy chair or bench where you can relax while watching birds at the feeder or butterflies sipping nectar from flowers. A couple of easy-to-use field guides always come in handy, especially ones that are specific to your region and include color photography of birds or butterflies instead of illustrations. We keep several on hand and find them to be an essential tool for identifying the wildlife we see and for learning more about them. Rick also uses the guidebook as a simple journal: when he sees a new species, he notes the date next to its picture.

Keeping a wildlife journal can be both helpful and rewarding. You can keep it simple by recording all the species you see, noting in particular the first ones to arrive and the last to leave. Or you can add more detail by noting their favorite spots in the garden and which foods they like best at the feeders. Recording which plants birds, butterflies, or moths frequent and which ones they avoid can give you the valuable information you need to tailor your backyard habitat to suit wildlife's preferences more exactly. You might also write down your observations of a species' behavior or the activity at a nest box, enter predator incidents—and even jot down your thoughts about your daily encounters with winged wildlife.

THE POWER OF BINOCULARS

A good pair of binoculars can make the difference between feeling as if you're watching a movie from the back row of the theater and the sense that you've moved in close enough to see every detail. In many cases, an inexpensive pair designed for backyard viewing will do just fine. The bottom line is that you'll need to be able to focus quickly as well as at close range. And you'll want binoculars that offer enough magnification to bring details into view, but not so powerful that you have trouble keeping the image steady.

The way to tell if a pair of binoculars fits that description is by looking at two main numbers printed on the binoculars; for example 7 x 35. The first number indicates the degree of magnification: the larger the number, the greater the magnification. The second refers to the size of the lens opening, and once again, the larger the number, the more light passes through and the brighter the image. Binoculars that offer between 7x and 10x magnification with a lens opening between 35 and 45 work well for most backyard viewing.

Get
INVOLVED

It's hard to enjoy any show if you're not there. Get out in the garden often so that the wildlife in your backyard gets used to your presence. Go ahead and talk to the birds while filling the feeder (even if you don't see them), so they get used to your voice. And it's a good idea to fill your feeders at night so the birds have a ready supply first thing in the morning. In the summer, I often go out in the early morning and sit on the bench to eat breakfast while watching the birds at the feeder. When the weather's cooler, we eat our breakfast in the kitchen, so we can look out the window and watch the birds enjoying theirs.

I also try to make sure I save some gardening chores—hand-watering, weeding, or deadheading summer flowers—for the afternoon when butterflies and dragonflies are at their most active. And I especially enjoy inviting guests over for a summer dinner. The highlight is always the chance to view sphinx moths up close as they sip nectar from flowers like salvia and verbena.

Take the time to sit down and enjoy the performance. Sometimes you'll get lucky, and in a matter of minutes, you'll stumble upon a hummingbird quietly perched just a few feet away on an arbor. Or you'll see a dragonfly snatching an insect in midair or a butterfly basking on a stone. Other times, you'll have to play a game of patience as you silently wait for wildlife to come into view. Either way, the end result is always the same—a wildlife show worth seeing again and again.

Don't park a bench in an out-of-the-way location on barren ground. Get right in the middle of the action by placing it beneath a tree and surrounding it with lush ground covers and plants.

133

Chapter 9

WILDLIFE PROFILES

These selected wildlife profiles will help you get up close and personal with some of the winged creatures that may come into your yard. For the most part, I chose to include species that were most likely to visit backyards in different parts of the United States and Canada. The descriptions in these profiles will help you determine just who your backyard guests are. Is the bird over there a black-capped, Carolina, or mountain chickadee? Was that a familiar bluet damselfly or a blue dasher dragonfly that just soared by? You'll also find information about their specific needs that you can use to create an inviting habitat for all kinds of winged wildlife. So read and enjoy.

**Black-headed grosbeak
(*Pheucticus melanocephalus*)**

Flame skimmer dragonfly (*Libellula saturata*)

**Pipevine swallowtail butterfly
(*Battus philenor*)**

Bird Profiles

Western bluebird *(Sialia mexicana)*

BLUEBIRD

With its brilliant blue plumage and a melodious song that heralds in spring, this "bluebird of happiness" is aptly named. As beneficial as it is beautiful, the bluebird gorges in spring and summer on large quantities of insects, from worms to grasshoppers.

Description

EASTERN BLUEBIRD *(Sialia sialis)*: males are striking, with brilliant blue above, chestnut underneath, and a white belly; females are duller and more muted.

WESTERN BLUEBIRD *(Sialia mexicana)*: males are similar to their eastern counterparts, but with deeper colors; the chestnut color underneath extends as scattered markings across its upper back; blue chin and throat; females are duller and more muted.

MOUNTAIN BLUEBIRD *(Sialia currucoides)*: males are turquoise blue—a deeper shade above and paler below, with a whitish belly; females are duller and more muted.

Range

Eastern bluebird: generally east of the U.S. Rockies and in southern Canada.

Western bluebird: southern British Columbia south to Baja, spreading across the western and southwestern United States to west Texas.

Mountain bluebird: throughout the western half of North America.

How to Attract

• Plant fruit-bearing trees and bushes, such as blueberry, elderberry, dogwood, holly, or sumac; offer diced fruit, berries, grapes, or chopped peanuts on a platform feeder; provide an extra treat with berry or insect suet.

• Place a nest box four to eight feet above the ground, preferably on a tree stump or wooden fence post, with an entrance hole 1½ inches in diameter; offer nesting materials, such as soft grasses, feathers, and hair; in the wild, builds nests in natural tree cavities and abandoned woodpecker holes; tough competition from foreign invaders, such as starlings and house sparrows, and loss of natural habitat have made natural nesting cavities harder to come by.

Painted bunting *(Passerina ciris)*

BUNTINGS

These finch-like neotropical migrants (species that spend winters in the tropics) are as colorful as parrots, as aggressive as jays, and as flighty as mourning doves. They bring more to the garden than just good looks—their lively, sweet chatter is enough to brighten anyone's day.

Description

INDIGO BUNTING *(Passerina cyanea)*: in bright sunlight males are a shimmering, deep ocean blue all over, sporting a small black patch around the bill and a bluish grape crown; plumage looks nearly black under poor light conditions; after molting, the male looks more like the brown female, except for a scattering of blue patches on the wings and tail.

LAZULI BUNTING *(Passerina amoena)*: males have a bright, turquoise-blue head; upperparts punctuated by two dazzling white wing bars, with touches of black on the wings and tail; white belly with a light cinnamon breast; females are soft brown above and lighter below, with a light wash of parakeet blue on the wings and tail.

PAINTED BUNTING *(Passerina ciris)*: males have blue-violet heads accented by red eye rings; a yellow-and-green back and bright red below; females are bright green above and yellow-green below.

Range

Indigo bunting: in North America, generally east of the U.S. Rockies—from the Gulf Coast up to southern Canada.

Lazuli bunting: from British Columbia to southern California, and east to North Dakota and central Texas.

Painted bunting: along the U.S. Atlantic coast from North Carolina to Florida and north from the Gulf Coast states to southern Kansas and Missouri.

How to Attract

• Supply seeds with plants like echinacea, cosmos, sunflowers, and zinnias as well as asters, goldenrod, and grasses; provide a fresh berry source by including shrubs and vines that produce fall fruits; stock feeding stations with sunflower, safflower, thistle, or millet; may also be attracted to peanuts, chopped fruits, and berries as well as suet feeders.

• Provide materials like grasses, leaves, bark strips, and twigs for nests and fine grasses, cotton, small roots, or hair for nest lining; in the wild, buntings build woven nests near the ground, usually in a cane thicket or in the fork of a bush or shrub.

Black-capped chickadee
(Parus atricapillus)

CHICKADEES

Chickadees are perky, playful, and quite the acrobats, hanging upside down while clinging to feeders or to the twigs of trees and shrubs. Opportunists, they feast on small insects and caterpillars and then on seeds and berries once insects become scarce. Of the six North American species, the most recognized are listed below.

Description

BLACK-CAPPED CHICKADEE *(Parus atricapillus)*: distinctive black cap and throat patch with extended white cheeks; narrow white edges to wing feathers; variable amounts of buff color on the flanks.

CAROLINA CHICKADEE *(Parus carolinensis)*: distinctive black cap and throat patch with extended white cheeks; the lower edge of black throat patch is more clearly defined than on other species; brown upperparts, light below; variable amounts of buff color on the flanks.

MOUNTAIN CHICKADEE *(Parus gambeli)*: distinctive black cap and throat patch with extended white cheeks; a white stripe above its eyes; overall coloration leans toward gray; a variable amount of pale gray on the flanks.

Range

Black-capped chickadee: northern two-thirds of the continental United States, plus much of Canada and Alaska.

Carolina chickadee: the southeastern United States and parts of the Midwest.

Mountain chickadee: western United States and Canada.

How to Attract

• Plant fruit-bearing trees and shrubs; grow seed favorites like pine, birch, hemlock, and sunflowers; fill feeders with sunflower seeds in addition to peanuts and fresh or dried berries; furnish a suet feeder.

• Place enclosed nest boxes 5 to 15 feet above the ground with entrance holes measuring 1⅛ inches in diameter. Chickadees are unusual in that they are the only backyard bird (besides woodpeckers) known to dig out their own nesting hole in natural cavities, such as an old woodpecker hole, in rotten wood, or a dead tree. So make your nest box more appealing by placing sawdust or wood chips in the bottom so they're fooled into thinking the cavity is newly excavated. Supply wool, feathers, fur, moss, and other soft materials for nest lining.

Mourning dove *(Zenaida macroura)*

Purple finch *(Carpodacus purpureus)*

DOVES

Of the eight species of doves that breed in North America, the mourning dove *(Zenaida macroura)* is the most recognized and one of the most widely distributed. It is also perhaps one of the most beautiful, with coloring that calls to mind the soft hues of a winter landscape. It possesses an equally gentle song that sounds like mournful cooing.

Description

MOURNING DOVE

(Zenaida macroura): fawn-colored head and chest with varying hues of brown on its back; gray patches on its head and nape; long, tapering tail; neck lightly brushed with iridescent pink and green; black spots on wings and tail. Females are not quite as colorful, lacking as they do the iridescent pink and green on the neck.

Range

Mourning dove: throughout the continental United States and southern Canada; a large number still migrate southward for winter.

How to Attract

• Offer seed favorites like millet, sunflower, cracked corn, milo, and thistle; they will frequent ground feeders or forage for seed spilled from hanging feeders.

• Plant a variety of trees and shrubs, especially evergreens, that will supply them with sticks for nest-building; mourning doves also use grass, forbs (nongrass herbs), and small roots to line their nests; in the wild, they usually build a platform of twigs lined with grass and small roots about 10 to 25 feet above the ground in trees, shrubs, or in vines; both parents take turns incubating the eggs, the male by day and the female by night.

• Be sure to offer a water source at or near ground level where they can drink and bathe.

FINCHES

Finches, with their colorful plumage, are lively, gregarious, and sociable. A delight to watch, they gather in large flocks unless it's breeding season. It's not uncommon to see hungry flocks of 20 or more descending upon backyard feeding stations.

Description

PURPLE FINCH *(Carpodacus purpureus)*: raspberry-red males, with color most intense on the head and at the crown.

HOUSE FINCH *(Carpodacus mexicanus)*: orange-red or, occasionally, yellow males; brown markings, a brown cap, and a streaked chest and belly.

CASSIN'S FINCH *(Carpodacus cassinii)*: largest of the three red-colored finches; males are a paler shade of rosy-red with a white chest; belly streaked with color; red-colored females lack the vibrant coloring of the males and look more like song sparrows.

AMERICAN GOLDFINCH *(Carduelis tristis)*: males are mostly a brownish gray in winter, but change to a bright yellow plumage in spring; black forehead; white edges on back wings and tail; females are a dull olive brown, other than a patch of white beneath, and have brown and black wings.

LESSER GOLDFINCH (*Carduelis psaltria*): males have black or green backs, with more pronounced white patches on wings than the American goldfinch; females are similar to males, only duller and lacking the black cap.

Range

Purple finch: throughout the eastern half of the United States, along the West Coast states, and in Canada from British Columbia east to Newfoundland.

House finch: throughout the western United States down into Texas, and in the eastern third of the country.

Cassin's finch: from southwestern Canada south through the western third of the United States.

American goldfinch: throughout the continental United States and southern Canada.

Lesser goldfinch: western United States, including areas of Colorado and Texas.

How to Attract

• Fill backyard feeders with seeds, especially sunflower or thistle; also eats millet along with suet and bread products; all species also eat a few buds in spring, insects in summer, and berries in fall.

• Supply nesting materials, such as grasses, fine twigs, mosses, hair, thistle or cattail down, and feathers; in the wild, nests usually consist of tightly woven cups made of grasses and fine twigs lined with mosses, fine grass, hair, and sometimes feathers; on occasion, house finch builds its nest in hanging baskets and is the only species known to use standard nest boxes with an entrance hole between 1¾ and 2½ inches in diameter, sometimes taking over purple martin houses; American goldfinch typically lines its nest with the down from thistle and sometimes cattail.

Black-headed grosbeak (*Pheucticus melanocephalus***)**

GROSBEAKS

Generally stocky birds about the size of robins, grosbeaks are more sophisticated and deliberate than their gregarious finch relatives. Each of the four most familiar species is quite distinctive in appearance, although they all have thick, oversized conical bills.

Description

EVENING GROSBEAK
(*Coccothraustes vespertinus)*: at first glance, it might be mistaken for a larger version of its close relative, the American goldfinch; distinguished by a characteristic oversized bill, smoky-yellow head and back, and black crown with a bright yellow forehead; females have a gray head and throat, with similar but softer versions of the colors found on males.

ROSE-BREASTED GROSBEAK
(Pheucticus ludovicianus): males have a black head and back with a white belly and an eye-catching red triangle on their breast; females look more like an overgrown sparrow and have prominent white eyebrows.

BLACK-HEADED GROSBEAK
(Pheucticus melanocephalus): males have a black head with white patches

on their black wings and tail; an autumn-orange nape and breast; females are similar to males, only with a lighter colored head and chest.

BLUE GROSBEAK (*Guiraca caerulea*): males are an iridescent deep blue with two chestnut-colored wing bars on black-tipped wings; females are a soft fawn color with two buff-colored wing bars.

Range

Evening grosbeak: throughout the continental United States and southern Canada.

Rose-breasted grosbeak: the northern United States, mainly east of the Great Plains; in Canada from northeastern British Columbia and then eastward to southern Alberta.

Black-headed grosbeak: western half of the United States and southwest corner of Canada.

Blue grosbeak: most of the United States, excluding the upper northern states and the Pacific Northwest.

How to Attract

• Fill feeders with sunflower seeds, though they also enjoy safflower or millet seeds as well as fruit and occasionally peanuts; plant conifers with seed-bearing cones, such as spruce and pine, as well as berry-producing trees and shrubs, like elderberries, hawthorn, box elder, winterberry, blackberries, and cherries; feeds on insects and fruit along with a wide mix of seeds.

• Supply twigs, grasses, plant fibers, small roots, and leaves; often nests in suburban yards, if small trees and shrubs provide adequate cover; nests usually consist of loosely woven plant materials lined with grasses and small roots and placed 5 to 25 feet high in a shrub or tree.

A female rufous hummingbird
(*Selasphorus rufous*)

HUMMINGBIRDS

Don't be fooled by their petite size. Hummingbirds possess a bold personality and extraordinary capabilities. As skilled avian acrobats, they can quickly maneuver in any direction, including backwards, stop on a dime, and hover in midair. They move through the air at incredible speeds and dive at up to 60 miles per hour. Nearly a third of their weight consists of flight muscles. At 60 to 80 wing beats per second, the wing beats of these energetic fliers surpass those of any songbird. As a result, their heart rate can soar to 1,220 beats per minute while flying. All that output of energy requires a massive input of fuel: hummers typically feed every 10 to 15 minutes throughout the day just to keep their strength up. Hummingbirds are exclusive to the Americas; however, only 14 of the 320 species are found in North America. All hummers have colorful, iridescent plumage. Only males possess an exceedingly brilliant throat patch, called a gorget, which looks like the scales found on the hood of medieval armor.

Description

RUBY-THROATED HUMMINGBIRD (*Archilochus colubris*): males have an iridescent green body; ruby red gorget; females are light green above with a white throat and breast.

BLACK-CHINNED HUMMINGBIRD (*Archilochus alexandri*): males have an iridescent green body; a black gorget underlined with purple-violet; females are green above, with buff-colored sides and a white throat.

RUFOUS HUMMINGBIRD (*Selasphorus rufous*): males have a rust-colored body except for a white breast; orange-red gorget; females are green above, with a rust-colored body, a white throat spotted with green, and patches of white on the belly.

ANNA'S HUMMINGBIRD (*Calypte anna*): males have an iridescent green body; magenta gorget; females have a green back and a grayish white belly and throat.

CALLIOPE (*Stellula calliope*): males have an iridescent green body; white gorget; females are green above and white below.

Range

Ruby-throated hummingbird: the eastern half of North America, from southern Canada to the Gulf Coast.

Black-chinned hummingbird: from British Columbia south and then east into central Texas.

Rufous hummingbird: much of northwest North America.

Anna's hummingbird: the Pacific seaboard, from British Columbia south and then east to Arizona.

Calliope: from interior British Columbia south to Colorado and west to the Pacific Coast mountains.

How to Attract

• Feature a variety of colorful nectar-rich flowers; offer several sugar water feeders at varying heights, preferably hanging near a patch of red flowers; tie several red ribbons on the poles where the feeders hang.

• Provide perching areas within easy access of nectar sources so they can stop and rest between feedings.

• Grow plants with fuzzy foliage or seeds, such as lamb's ears or cattails, so hummers can harvest the downy fibers for their nests; nests are composed of soft plant material held together with strands of sticky spider web and covered with lichens; a single golf ball could fill a hummer's delicate, compact nest, which has an average outer diameter of only 1½ inches.

Blue jays *(Cyanocitta cristata)*

JAYS

These big, bold dynamic birds are curious and intelligent to a fault. What they lack in backyard manners, they more than make up for with their attractive beauty and good-natured charm.

Description

BLUE JAY *(Cyanocitta cristata)*: bright blue feathering; a white mask with black facial markings; white belly; spectacular blue crest, black ring around the neck, and black bars traversing the wings and tail.

STELLER'S JAY *(Cyanocitta stelleri)*: handsome black crest, with black extending down the front parts; rest of the body is cobalt blue.

SCRUB JAY

(Aphelocoma coerulescens): a dusky blue head, breast band, wings, and tail; dark mask, soft gray back, and a nearly white underbelly and throat.

Range

Blue jay: east of the U.S. Rockies and in southern Canada.

Steller's jay: most of the area in both the United States and Canada between the Rockies and the Pacific Coast, including coastal Alaska.

Scrub jay: a split range, with a large population in the western United States from southern Washington south to Texas and an isolated group in central Florida.

How to Attract

• Be sure to include plant foods in the form of fruit-bearing trees and shrubs, as well as nut-bearing trees or even an oak tree for acorns; stock a backyard feeder with sunflower seeds, cracked corn, bread products, and, especially, raw peanuts.

• Often nests in yards but not in birdhouses, so plant a variety of trees, shrubs, and vines to interest neighborhood jays in setting up house; meet their nest-building needs by offering a pile of sticks and twigs as well as a mud source nearby; also offer the moss, dry grasses, fine roots, and hair used to line nests.

Dark-eyed junco *(Junco hyemalis)*

JUNCOS

Although juncos are one of the most familiar birds at winter feeders, sometimes all it takes is leaf-covered ground to attract these sparrow-sized birds to your yard. Like hungry chickens, these birds scavenge the ground, scooting backwards with both feet to scratch out a meal of seeds or insects. And, like chickens, there's a pecking order among these birds, with the most dominant roosting at top. At one time, dark-eyed juncos *(Junco hyemalis)* were actually divided into several different species, but due to interbreeding where ranges overlapped, they are now considered to be one species subdivided into races or strains. As a result, this familiar backyard visitor can be highly variable in appearance. Females of all strains are similar to males, only more muted in color. The ranges given below for the individual strains are where they are most commonly, but not exclusively, found. For example, the gray-headed strain, most frequently found in the southwestern United States, can also be spotted in Oregon. The four most common strains are listed here.

Description

WESTERN OREGON STRAIN *(Junco hyemalis)*: a charcoal to black hood, cinnamon-colored back and sides, and a soft grayish white belly.

PINK-SIDED STRAIN *(Junco hyemalis)*: similar to the Oregon variety, but with a grayish hood and pinkish sides.

SLATE-COLORED STRAIN *(Junco hyemalis)*: slate gray above and white below.

GRAY-HEADED STRAIN *(Junco hyemalis)*: a slate gray overall with a rust-colored patch on its back.

Range

Western Oregon strain: west from the Sierra Nevada and Cascade mountain ranges.

Pink-sided strain: found in the U.S. Rockies.

Slate-colored strain: found in the northern and eastern United States; in much of the eastern United States, appears only in winter.

Gray-headed strain: most common in the southwestern United States.

How to Attract

• Grow plants that are good sources of seeds, like goldenrod, purple coneflower, sunflowers, asters, cosmos and zinnias; generally prefers to feed on the ground and will clean up seeds that have fallen beneath a feeder, will also eat from a low platform feeder or hanging feeder when filled with seed favorites like sunflower or millet; may also accept finely cracked corn, rolled oats, or chopped peanuts.

• Supply grass, moss, strips of bark, twigs, small roots, and hair for nests; nests are usually located in a concealed spot on the ground, in brush piles, in tree roots, under fallen logs, or occasionally on slopes or banks protected by low-growing shrubs and bushes.

White-breasted nuthatch *(Sitta carolinensis)*

NUTHATCHES

These tiny, wedge-shaped birds are more detail-oriented than accountants, scrutinizing every nook and cranny in trees for grubs, ants, and other tasty insects. Their nimble nature gives them the ability to forage headfirst down trees, creeping along trunks and branches as they search in crevices and beneath loose bark for food. Still, nuthatches are always on the lookout, even when clinging upside-down to a tree. With an upward tilt of the head, both bill and breast become fully horizontal so it can keep a watchful eye on its surroundings. Although several species are found throughout North America, the two best known are listed. Of the two, red-breasted nuthatches are more widespread, though the larger white-breasted is the better known.

Description

WHITE-BREASTED NUTHATCH *(Sitta carolinensis)*: stocky with stubby tail and gray feathering on back; a black stripe on the head running from the front to the back of the neck; white face and belly.

RED-BREASTED NUTHATCH *(Sitta canadensis)*: stocky with stubby tail and gray feathering on back; black stripe on the head running front to back; light cinnamon belly and a prominent black eye line.

Range

White-breasted nuthatch and the **red-breasted nuthatch**: throughout much of North America at various times of the year, except in extreme northern Canada and the southern sections of Texas and Florida.

How to Attract

• Provide feeders stocked with sunflower seeds, cracked corn, or nuts; also appreciates suet feeders in winter; feeds on tree seeds and insects found on bark, so grow nut trees and conifers, like pine, spruce, and fir.

• Offer nest boxes with a 1¼-inch diameter hole, placed 10 to 20 feet above the ground, as well as a ready supply of nesting materials, such as grass, small roots, moss, hair, fur, and feathers; in the wild, seeks out natural cavities in trees or will take over a former woodpecker cavity, so establish nesting sites by growing trees and conifers.

American robin *(Turdus migratorius)*

ROBINS

With so many poems, stories, and songs starring the robin, this delightful bird is a celebrity. One song in particular, "Rockin' Robin," describes the bird dance they perform while searching for worms: a hop-and-stop step done while cocking their heads from side to side until they spy a worm and snatch their reward.

Description

AMERICAN ROBIN *(Turdus migratorius)*: charcoal above, with a nearly black head and tail; rusty red breast; white eye rings set off its black eyes.

Range

American robin: throughout most of Canada and the continental United States.

White-crowned sparrow
(*Zonotrichia leucophrys*)

SPARROWS

The unassuming sparrow may easily go unnoticed. In general, they have light undersides with brown and/or gray uppersides and are often streaked all over in shades of black, brown, and gray. Yet its subtle beauty—with its complex patterns and blending of shades—looks as if an artist hand-painted each one. Add to that its melodious song and fondness for feeders, and this easy-going bird certainly deserves a second look. Female sparrows are similar to males, though sometimes a bit more muted in color. Listed below are the species most likely to appear as backyard guests.

Description

SONG SPARROW (*Melospiza melodia*): heavily streaked all over, with a gray stripe above its eye; brown above and white below.

CHIPPING SPARROW (*Spizella passerina*): chestnut cap, gray below, and gray face with a black streak through the eye; tan above with dark streaks.

AMERICAN TREE SPARROW (*Spizella arborea*): a light gray belly; tan back with dark streaks; chestnut cap, eye streak, and blotch on its gray chest.

WHITE-CROWNED SPARROW (*Zonotrichia leucophrys*): gray below and tan above with dark streaks; a gray face; alternating black and white stripes on the head.

WHITE-THROATED SPARROW (*Zonotrichia albicollis*): yellow in front of the eye, with alternating black and white stripes on the head; dark-streaked, brown above, a dull white to grayish tan chest and belly, and, of course, a white throat.

Range

Song sparrow and **chipping sparrow:** throughout the United States and much of Canada.

American tree sparrow: summers in Alaska and northern Canada; winters anywhere from southern Canada to the central United States.

White-crowned sparrow: western third of North America and northern Canada; winters in much of the southern United States.

White-throated sparrow: western North America, the southern half of the United States, and the northern half of Canada.

How to Attract

• Fill feeders placed on the ground or platform feeders with seed favorites, such as sunflower and millet, as well as safflower, thistle, cracked corn, canary seed and bread products; birds will forage for seed underneath feeders; also grow fruiting shrubs like cotoneaster, viburnums, roses, and heavenly bamboo.

• Supply feathers, hair, fur, grasses, weeds, bark, twigs, and moss, so they can build and line nests; in the wild, nests are usually in remote or well-hidden locations, including brush piles.

How to Attract

• Increase the earthworm population by creating a brush pile or a mound of garden debris; plant berry bushes and other fruit-bearing trees, shrubs, and vines; stock a feeder with apples, cherries, grapes, and soaked raisins, as well as other berries and dried fruits.

• Offer an open nesting shelf that provides overhead protection; in the wild, robins use grasses and mud to construct cup-shaped nests (female coats inner bowls by spreading mud with her breast), so make sure there are plenty of mud puddles during the spring and summer mating season; nests usually placed in the fork of a tree or shrub, anywhere from on the ground up to 50 feet high; also utilizes windowsills or ledges.

Tree swallow *(Tachycineta bicolor)*

SWALLOWS

When it comes to avian performers, swallows are among the most entertaining to watch. These skillful fliers put on a fantastic aerial display, executing split-second maneuvers while catching bugs on the wing. As early evening approaches, they become even more animated, darting about during a feeding-frenzy in the sky. There's an added bonus: one swallow can easily devour hundreds of garden pests a day, and at dusk they sweep the skies for mosquitoes. The most widespread and widely recognized of the North American species are listed below.

Description

BARN SWALLOW *(Hirundo rustica)*: deeply forked tail; males are cinnamon below and midnight blue above; females are similar to males, but colors are more muted.

TREE SWALLOW *(Tachycineta bicolor)*: males have a distinguished black mask; black wings, iridescent cobalt blue back and head; white belly and throat; females are the same as males, only slightly duller.

VIOLET-GREEN SWALLOW *(Tachycineta thalassina)*: males are snow white below; white cheeks; metallic green and violet above; green crown and back, with violet wings and tail; females are a muted version of the male, with less white on the face.

PURPLE MARTIN *(Progne subis)*: deep purple to black overall; females are deep purple to black, with grayish white underneath.

Range

Barn swallow: throughout the continental United States (not including Florida) and most of Canada.

Tree swallow: most of the United States and Canada, wintering in the southern regions of the United States, from North Carolina west to southern California.

Violet-green swallow: throughout western North America, from the Rocky Mountains west to the Pacific Coast.

Purple martin: mostly east of the U.S. Rockies, with a scattering on the West Coast; also in the central interior of Canada.

How to Attract

• Grow fruit-bearing trees and shrubs that produce early in the season, such as dogwood, holly, bayberry, and winterberry; diet consists mostly of insects (barn swallows and purple martins exclusively so), with up to 30 percent of their diet in winter and early spring consisting of fruits and berries.

• Generally returns year after year to the same nest located in a tree cavity, an abandoned woodpecker hole, or frequently, in a nest box; barn swallows are the exception, building mud nests they plaster under eaves or on beams in barns, sheds, or in other outdoor buildings; offer most swallows nest boxes with entrance holes of 1¼ to 1½ inches in diameter, placed 5 to 15 feet above the ground; however, purple martins require larger openings, in the 1¾- to 2½ inch range. Both barn swallows and purple martins nest in colonies; barn swallows prefer open-topped bowl nests, like that provided by half a coconut shell; offer purple martins colony-type birdhouses east of the U.S. Rockies and gourd houses in the West.

Eastern towhee *(Pipilo erythrophthalmus)*

TOWHEES

The robin-like towhees of the East and West were once known as the rufous-sided towhee. Due to geographical variations in song and their distinctive plumage, the rufous-sided towhee was split into two separate species—the eastern towhee and the spotted towhee of the western United States and southern portions of western Canada.

Description

EASTERN TOWHEE *(Pipilo erythrophthalmus)*: with its rusty sides, it looks like a more dramatic version of a robin, only smaller and more slender, with a white breast; black head, back, and wings in males; brown head, back, and wings in females.

SPOTTED TOWHEE *(Pipilo maculatus)*: black head; black back and wings with white spots in males, paler in females; rusty sides and a white belly.

GREEN-TAILED TOWHEE *(Pipilo chlororus)*: rusty red cap, white throat, and gray body dipped in olive-yellow on the wings and back; bears no resemblance to the other towhees; females are similar to males.

Range

Eastern towhee: resides throughout much of the eastern third of the United States, extending its winter range west to Texas and Kansas and its summer range north to the Great Lake states and southern New England.

Spotted towhee: from British Columbia south into the western United States.

Green-tailed towhee: from central Oregon south through the mountains to southern California, with some wintering as far east as southern Texas.

How to Attract

• Because towhees are ground feeders that search in thick cover for insects and seeds that make up most of their diet, strew millet and sunflower seeds on the ground or place feeders there; will also often accept cracked corn and peanuts and usually forages beneath hanging feeders for spilled seeds. Include cotoneasters or other low-lying, berry-producing shrubs.

• Provide protective cover in the form of a variety of small shrubs and bushes; they typically build nests on or near the ground, usually in a clump of grass, beneath a small bush, or in a low shrub; grasses, twigs, weeds, leaves, and bark strips are most often used to build the nest, which they then line with finer materials like grasses, bark shreds, small roots, and hair.

House wren *(Troglodytes aedon)*

WRENS

Animated and industrious to a fault, these little balls of energy are exceptional bug eaters. By consuming insects on the ground or in bushes and shrubs, they control the pest population in your garden. These short-tailed birds vary in color from light to dark in shades of brown and gray. As somewhat plain-looking brown birds, wrens often go unnoticed. Yet these songsters belt out some of the most delightful summer songs. Of the nine species found in North America, the four most prevalent are listed below.

Description

HOUSE WREN
(Troglodytes aedon): basic brown with lighter brown markings on the tail and wings.

WINTER WREN
(Troglodytes troglodytes): similarly unadorned, but at 4 inches long is smaller and darker than the house wren and has a shorter tail.

CAROLINA WREN
(Thryothorus ludovicianus): rusty above; white throat; buff-colored below; conspicuous white eyebrow.

BEWICK'S WREN
(Thryomanes bewickii): gray-brown to brown above, a grayish white breast

and belly; white corners on its fan-shaped tail.

Range

House wren: most of the continental United States and parts of Canada.

Winter wren: in the United States from Alaska south to California, in the Northeast and Great Lakes region and throughout southern portions of Canada; winters across much of the southern United States.

Carolina wren: mainly south from the Great Lakes region of the United States and then west to Texas.

Bewick's wren: a band from southern British Columbia through California, across the southern United States and up to southern Ontario.

How to Attract

• Make insect smorgasbords by leaving wood piles and brush heaps in corners of the yard; since they are primarily insect eaters, they don't usually frequent feeders, but they often find suet appealing.

• Grow a variety of shrubs and bushes to offer cover and create additional places to feed; set up several birdhouses with entrance holes measuring between 1 and 1½ inches in diameter, depending on the species; nest boxes are also commonly used for roosting as well as nesting; in the wild, wrens build in anything from a natural tree cavity, an old woodpecker hole, and a crevice in a stone wall to a hanging basket, coat pocket, outdoor boots, or even an open tin can.

Eastern-tailed blue butterfly (Everes comyntas)

BLUES

Male blues have wings in shades of shimmering blue above and grayish white to nearly white with specks of black below. Females are more muted in color, with some displaying more brown than blue tones. Color tone and intensity can vary, depending on the species and time of year, with some spring adults more vividly colored than in summer. The wingspans of most species of this petite butterfly average 1 inch. As part of the gossamer wing family (Lycaenidae), blues appear carefree when in flight, though they are easily startled when resting. Their elusive nature only heightens the excitement of those rare times when you have the chance to see one up close. Caterpillars may be yellow, green, yellow-green, or even pink—some sporting thin, colorful stripes or covered in fine white hairs.

Description

EASTERN-TAILED BLUE *(Everes comyntas)*: wings with narrow black borders framed by white fringe and with orange markings on the hindwing near the tail; pale gray underneath.

WESTERN-TAILED BLUE *(Everes amyntula)*: wings with narrow black borders framed by white fringe, with orange markings on the hindwing near the tails; nearly white underneath.

BOISDUVAL'S BLUE *(Icaricia icarioides)*: striking with an intense shade of blue above.

SPRING AZURE *(Celastrina argiolus)*: a subtle blue above, with males lacking black borders.

Range

Eastern-tailed blue: throughout the eastern two-thirds of North America.

Western-tailed blue: western North America, sweeping east along the U.S.-Canadian border to the Great Lakes region.

Boisduval's blue: west of the U.S. Rockies and southern Canada.

Spring azure: throughout most of North America, but uncommon in Florida and the far North.

Life Cycle

Most blues overwinter as larvae, though spring azures survive winter as pupae. Blues complete their cycle from egg to butterfly in four to seven weeks.

When to Observe

Blues are typically observed early spring through fall in the northern part of their range, and late winter to late fall in the southern part; Boisduval's blue can be seen from mid-spring through summer.

How to Attract

• Plant flowering clovers and various legumes to serve as host plants for most species; in addition, plant willows, dogwood, viburnum, spirea, sumacs, milkweed, and various hollies for spring azures, as well as lupines for Boisduval's blue caterpillars.

• Plant flowering nectar sources for adults, such as those in the daisy or buckwheat families; flowering herbs like lavender, rosemary, thyme, and mints, as well as flowering clovers and legumes. Blues are "puddlers," so including a mud puddle or two will attract their attention.

Great spangled fritillary on a zinnia
(Speyeria cybele)

FRITILLARIES

This group of highly patterned butterflies includes both the greater fritillaries, with wingspans generally measuring 2 to 3¾ inches, and the lesser fritillaries, with wingspans of only 1½ to 2 inches. Most adult butterflies are bright orange to orange-brown above with black "checkered" spots. Caterpillars are generally black with large barbed spines that act as a protective defense against predators such as birds. The similar gulf fritillary (*Agraulis vanillae*) is actually not a true fritillary but is instead a member of the longwing family, along with the zebra butterfly.

Description

GREAT SPANGLED *(Speyeria cybele)*: males are tan to orange with black "checkered" spots above; noted especially for its underwing pattern of flashy silver spots that "spangle," or sparkle, in sunlight; females are paler than males, with bolder, dark markings on the wings.

REGAL *(Speyeria idalia)*: bright orange-red above with black "checkered" spots on the forewings; white spots on black hindwings; males also have orange spots on hindwings.

MEADOW *(Boloria bellona)*: orange-red with heavy black markings above, though it lacks dark outer margins found on other fritillaries.

HYDASPE *(Speyeria hydaspe)*: orange-brown above with heavy black spots.

Range

Great spangled: most common and widespread of the larger fritillaries; most of the United States (except the Deep South) and in southern Canada.

Regal: declining numbers; formerly found east of the U.S. Rockies; now found in the tall grass prairie of the Midwest.

Meadow: northern United States and from eastern British Columbia through southern Canada.

Hydaspe: western United States, from southern California east to New Mexico and then northward into southern Canada, from Alberta west to British Columbia.

Life Cycle

All species share similar life cycles. Adult females commonly lay eggs in late summer, with caterpillars hatching in fall and hibernating through winter. Once spring arrives, the caterpillars gorge on violets for several weeks. They then complete their cycle by spending from one to three weeks in the pupal phase before emerging as winged adults.

When to Observe

Sightings of fritillaries vary among species and regions, from May to October. The great spangled fritillary can be seen from late spring through fall.

How to Attract

• Plant violets in a partially shaded location to serve as host plants for caterpillars.

• Plant butterfly bushes, clover, and flowers in the composite family—black-eyed Susans, purple coneflower, or zinnias for example—to supply nectar for adults.

Monarch butterfly (Danaus plexippus)

MONARCHS

One of the most beloved and best known of American butterflies, monarchs belong to the milkweed family of butterflies (Danaidae), which also includes the queen and viceroy. Monarchs are unique in that they're the only truly migratory butterfly. Their migratory habits vary according to where they make their home: monarchs from Canada and the eastern United States generally migrate to the mountains of Mexico while those in the Far West typically overwinter along the California coast.

This annual mass migration is an extraordinary event, to say the least. Each fall, hundreds of millions of monarchs leave on a journey that can cover several thousand miles. Resembling hanging clusters of stained glass, they spend their winters massed on the trunks and branches of pines, eucalyptus, and other trees. During this state of inactivity, they survive on fat reserves stored in their bodies. Most monarchs mate just before leaving their wintering grounds, depositing eggs on milkweed plants in spring during their northern trek.

Description

MONARCH (Danaus plexippus): pumpkin orange wings with black veining; black margins on wings marked with white spots; wingspan of 3½ to 4 inches; black head and body bearing a few white spots; colorful caterpillars marked with alternating bands of black, white, and yellow.

Range

Monarch: summers spent throughout the continental United States and southern Canada; winters spent in Mexico or along the California coast.

Life Cycle

Monarchs produce up to six broods a year in the South and four broods a year in the North. Adults that migrate southward may live up to seven months or more; others live one to three months, depending on the time of year. Complete metamorphosis from egg to butterfly generally occurs in about four weeks.

When to Observe

Monarchs are generally seen from May to October, with fall migration beginning as early as August.

How to Attract

• Grow milkweed family plants, such as butterfly weed to attract egg-laying females and feed caterpillars.

• Plant a variety of nectar flowers for adults, including butterfly bush, lilac, goldenrod, lantana, purple coneflower, and sedums, as well as asters, liatris or blazing star, verbena, cosmos, and zinnias; fill a butterfly fruit feeder with watermelon slices.

Mourning cloak *(Nymphalis antiopa)*

MOURNING CLOAKS

Picture a traditional, somber mourning cloak worn by someone hundreds of years ago, and you'll see the resemblance to the mourning cloak butterfly (*Nymphalis antiopa*). However, sorrow certainly doesn't come to mind when you see this charmer fluttering in your garden. You might even catch sight of its beautiful wings, a harbinger of spring on a warm winter day.

Description

MOURNING CLOAK *(Nymphalis antiopa)*: striking and easily identifiable; a 3- to 4-inch wingspan; dark brown wings with pale borders below; beautiful dark mahogany above with creamy yellow edging flanked by bright blue dots set against a black border; intimidating caterpillar, with a black body spotted in red and covered with bristly spines and hairs.

Range

Mourning cloak: widespread throughout North America.

Life Cycle

Mourning cloaks may just be the longest living butterfly species in North America, with some living up to 11 months as adults. Their long adult life span is a result of two hibernations, called estivation, one in winter and one in summer. Adults from summer broods overwinter as butterflies in protected nooks and crannies. Butterflies emerge in early spring and soon lay their eggs. Once the eggs hatch, the caterpillars pupate, emerge as adults, and shortly afterwards, estivate until fall, when they feed once again before retiring for the winter.

When to Observe

Mourning cloaks are one of the first butterfly species to appear in spring; often seen feeding from tree sap; active from spring through fall; can be seen basking in the sun's rays on winter days when temperatures reach 60°F (15.6°C) or above.

How to Attract

• Grow host plant favorites, including willows, elms, birches, aspens, hackberries, and cottonwoods.

• Plant trees such as oaks, birches, and maples that provide tree sap for adults (adults rarely visit flowers). Place soft, overly ripe fruit in a butterfly fruit feeder. They also frequent mud puddles for added nutrients.

• Provide places for them to hibernate in winter, such as tree cavities, woodpiles, or loose tree bark.

American painted lady
(Vanessa virginiensis)

PAINTED LADIES

This classy group of cosmopolitan butterflies belongs to the subfamily of varied brushfoots (Nymphalinae), distinguished by their somewhat bushy forelegs that are smaller than their hindlegs. All painted ladies share similar markings of orange and black with tips spotted in white on the upperside of their wings. The attractive undersides reveal an intricate pattern of mostly gray, black, and white with pale agate and rose. The caterpillar is unassuming in appearance, yet spiny when mature. One of the most adaptable butterflies in the world, the painted lady exists on every continent except for Australia and Antarctica.

Description

PAINTED LADY *(Vanessa cardui)*: by far the largest and most widespread, with a 2- to 3-inch wingspan; orange-brown and black on the upperside, with black tips marked with white spots on the forewing; black, brown, and gray-patterned underside.

AMERICAN PAINTED LADY *(Vanessa virginiensis)*: slightly smaller, with a 1¾- to 2-inch wingspan; brown, yellow, orange, and black-patterned upperside;

black tips spotted in white; extra white spotting in the orange patch on its upperside; two large eyespots on undersides of wings.

WEST COAST LADY *(Vanessa annabella)*: 1½- to 2-inch wingspan; orange-brown and black upperside; distinguished by its four black-ringed, blue eyespots in the margins on the hindwing on either side of its tail.

Range

Painted lady: throughout North America.

American painted lady: throughout most of the continental United States and southern Canada.

West Coast lady: western North America, from British Columbia south.

Life Cycle

Depending on the season, the complete cycle from egg to butterfly can take from four to eight weeks. Most adults live between 6 to 20 days as butterflies.

When to Observe

Painted ladies can be seen all year in the southern part of their range; generally seen spring through fall in the North.

How to Attract

• Host plants favorites vary by species. For the painted lady, plant thistle (a special favorite), as well as composite and mallow family members, such as sunflowers and hollyhocks; the American painted lady lays eggs on members of the everlasting family, such as pearly everlasting, sweet everlasting, and pussytoes as well as other plants, such as forget-me-nots, artemisia, and burdock; West Coast lady favors mallows, including hollyhocks, musk mallow, and lavatera.

• Plant nectar plants for all species of adults, including the butterfly bush, asters, sunflowers, zinnias, cosmos, and chaste tree, as well as goldenrods, marigolds, pearly everlastings, and vetch; the painted lady especially favors thistles.

Fiery skipper on zinnia *(Hylephila phyleus)*

SKIPPERS

Take one look at these furry fliers, and it's easy to see why skippers are in a class by themselves. They share characteristics of both moths and butterflies, along with a few that are unique to the skipper family (Hesperiidae). Like butterflies, they fly by day. Their bodies, however, appear more like moths—stocky, with relatively large heads and short wingspans of ½ to 2 inches. Speedy fliers, they come equipped with streamlined wings and are noted for rapidly "skipping" about from flower to flower. While some skippers are quite unique, all have wings that are generally shades of brown, from tawny to russet and chocolate. One distinctive characteristic shared by all skippers are their eyes, which appear large in proportion to their size. Also unique are their antennae, which end in small hooks—unlike butterfly antennae that end with rounded knobs or the feathery or threadlike antennae of moths.

Description

SILVER-SPOTTED

(Epargyreus clarus): cocoa-colored wings, orange markings on the forewings, and large, silvery-white patches below; an approximately 1¾- to 2½-inch wingspan.

COMMON-CHECKERED (*Pyrgus communis*): an average 1-inch wingspan and a checkerboard design of taupe and white.

FIERY SKIPPER (*Hylephila phyleus*): chocolate brown, with yellow-orange markings and a 1½-inch wingspan.

JUBA (*Hesperia juba*): tawny orange above, with yellow-olive and white patches below; a wingspan of approximately 1¼ to 1½ inches.

LONG-TAILED (*Urbanus proteus*): arguably the most striking skipper of the North American species, with prominent, long tails; iridescent blue-green on the upperwings; a 1½- to 2-inch wingspan.

Range

Silver-spotted: scattered throughout most of North America, but most numerous east of the U.S. Rockies.

Common-checkered: widespread across the United States and then northward into Canada.

Fiery skipper: across the southern United States, with a few found as far north as southern Minnesota and New England.

Juba: western United States and the southern interior of British Columbia.

Long-tailed: mostly a southern species, with the largest populations found in the Southeast.

Life Cycle

Metamorphosis from egg to butterfly can take from 6 to 10 weeks, depending on the season, with adult butterflies living from 10 to 20 days. Different species overwinter in different phases of the life cycle. The silver-spotted skipper, for example, spends the winter as a larva, while the long-tailed skipper goes through winter as an adult.

When to Observe

Most skipper species can be seen throughout summer, with year-round appearances in the southern portions of their range. The long-tailed skipper is a southern species but ventures north.

How to Attract

• Host plants vary among species, although as a group, caterpillars mostly feed on grasses, sedges, and legumes like wisteria, peas, and beans; plants in the mallow family are favored by the common-checkered skipper.

• Plant a variety of nectar-rich flowers appealing to all species; choices include shrubs and vines, such as butterfly bush, bluebeard, chaste tree, lantana, lavender, and honeysuckle, as well as perennials and annuals, such as asters, eupatorium, goldenrod, ironweed, purple coneflower, sunflowers, salvias, sedums, or verbena.

Orange-barred sulphur (*Phoebis philea*)

SULPHURS

These medium-sized butterflies arrive early in spring. Belonging to the Pieridae family, sulphurs are mostly yellow or orange, with a translucent quality to their wings that makes them appear as delicate as bone china. With full-sized forelegs, they're quite adept at walking and are often seen gathering at mud puddles.

Description

CLOUDLESS SULPHUR

(*Phoebis sennae*): ranging in color from yellowish green to orange-yellow; wingspans from 2½ to 3 inches.

CLOUDED SULPHUR

(*Colias philodice*): smaller, with a 1½- to 2¾-inch wingspan; ornate black edging and salmon spots on lemon yellow wings.

ORANGE SULPHUR

(*Colias eurytheme*): ornate black edging and salmon spots on orange wings; wingspan of 1⅜ to 2¾ inches.

ORANGE-BARRED SULPHUR

(*Phoebis philea*): yellow-orange wings; a broad orange bar on the forewings; a 2¾- to 3¼-inch wingspan.

SLEEPY ORANGE

(*Eurema nicippe*): black markings, with wings that vary from tan to yellow to bright orange, depending on the region and season; wingspan of 1⅜ to 2 inches.

Cloudless sulphur: mostly in eastern North America.

Clouded and orange sulphurs: throughout most of North America.

Orange-barred sulphur: mostly in the southern United States.

Sleepy orange: mostly in the southern United States, though they may extend further north, up into the Great Lakes region.

Life Cycle

Depending on the species and time of year, life cycles can range from four to eight weeks, with some species wintering as larvae and others as adults.

When to Observe

Some species of sulphur appear early in spring; most northern species fly anywhere from spring through fall, with shorter periods farther north; southern species appear year-round.

How to Attract

• Plant a wide variety of legumes that will serve as host plants for most species; examples include clovers, alfalfa, vetch, astragalus, peas, and cassia.

• Feature an open area surrounded by a variety of nectar-rich flowers, including flowering herbs and clovers, along with a mud puddle where they can gather to drink; some species remain late into fall, so include fall-blooming flowers such as asters, goldenrod, chrysanthemums, purple coneflower, and sedums.

Western tiger swallowtail
(*Papilio rutulus*)

SWALLOWTAILS

When it comes to beauty, style, and grace, swallowtails (which belong to the Papilionidae family) are supreme among North American butterflies. Their large size, as well as their colorful stripes and dots, makes them an easy summer visitor to spot. Though they fly away quickly when disturbed, their more typical leisurely flight from flower to flower means you'll often have the chance to see this butterfly up close. Their wingspans range from 2½ to 5½ inches, from the smaller black, zebra, and anise swallowtails to the larger eastern tiger, western tiger, and giant swallowtails. Both their wing patterns and their coloring varies. Swallowtail caterpillars resemble small bird droppings when young but later their color changes to green—providing an effective camouflage for them when they are feeding on leaves. They also come equipped with a bizarre-looking orange, tongue-like, forked gland (called an osmeterium) that releases an offending smell when threatened; some also have eyespots (markings near the head that look like giant eyes), which make them appear more intimidating.

Description

EASTERN TIGER (*Papilio glaucus*), **WESTERN TIGER** (*Papilio rutulus*), and **ANISE SWALLOWTAILS** (*Papilio*

zelicaon): black body; black-and-yellow pattern on wings; a row of blue spots bordering the tail end.

BLACK SWALLOWTAIL
(*Papilio polyxenes*) and **GIANT SWALLOWTAILS** (*Papilio cresphontes*): black body; black with some yellow on wings.

PALE SWALLOWTAIL
(*Papilio eurymedon*): black body; pale cream-and-black stripes on wings; black border and long twisted tail.

ZEBRA SWALLOWTAIL
(*Eurytides marcellus*): black body; black-and-white or dark brown-and-white stripes with red markings at the base; a swordlike tail.

PIPEVINE SWALLOWTAIL
(*Battus philenor*): black body; black-and-blue wings lacking interior markings; underwings distinguished by a row of seven orange spots on a blue field.

SPICEBUSH SWALLOWTAIL
(*Papilio troilus*): black body; bluish black wings accented by an added row of prominent white dots; pale green spots on the underwings.

Range

Eastern tiger swallowtail: east of the U.S. Rockies and most of Canada.

Black swallowtail, spicebush swallowtail, and **giant swallowtail:** east of the U.S. Rockies and into southern Canada.

Anise swallowtail, pale swallowtail, and **western tiger swallowtail:** west of the U.S. Rockies; anise swallowtail also ventures into southwestern Canada.

Pipevine swallowtail: mostly in the eastern and southern United States, then sweeps across the South and proceeds up the West Coast into northern California.

Zebra swallowtail: most common in the South, with ranges extending into the eastern half of the United States and parts of Canada.

Life Cycle

Most swallowtails overwinter as pupae, some as partially grown caterpillars. Depending on the season, the complete cycle from egg to butterfly can take from six to ten weeks. Most adults live between 6 to 14 days as butterflies.

When to Observe

Swallowtails generally appear from May to September in the North; nearly year-round in the South.

How to Attract

• Host plant favorites vary by species. Plant dill, fennel, carrot, parsley, and other carrot-family members for black and anise swallowtail caterpillars; trees and shrubs such as aspens, willows, birches, ashes, cherries, lilac, and tulip trees in the East and poplars, alders, serviceberries, hawthorns, aspens, willows, and ashes in the West for tiger swallowtails; various citrus, along with common prickly ash, hop tree, and rue for giant swallowtails; alders, ceanothus, hawthorns, buckthorns, cherries, and plums for the pale swallowtail; pawpaws for the zebra; spicebush, sassafras and various bays for the spicebush; and pipevines for pipevine caterpillars.

• Plant a variety of nectar plants for adults, ranging from low-growing mints, verbena, and zinnias to taller shrubs and trees, like azaleas, milkweeds, honeysuckles, butterfly bush, and lilacs. They also frequent mud puddles.

Cabbage white butterfly on salvia
(*Pieris rapae*)

WHITES

These dainty, medium-sized butterflies are no less beautiful than other more brightly colored butterflies. Members of the Pieridae family, whites have 1½- to 2-inch wingspans. Some species exhibit several black or orange markings, with females usually displaying more extensive markings.

As early spring arrives, they are a welcome sight as they glide in a rollercoaster-like flight over the landscape.

Description

CHECKERED WHITE (*Pontia protodice*): scattered gray or black checkers on white wings; more prominent markings appearing in cooler weather.

WESTERN WHITE (*Pontia occidentalis*): scattered gray or black checkers on white wings; a greater concentration of gray markings near the forewing tip.

CABBAGE WHITE (*Pieris rapae*): lemon white wings and charcoal tips on the forewings; caterpillars are well camouflaged in shades of green to blue-green, some with black dots or yellow lines.

Range

Western white: mostly in the western part of North America, from Colorado north to Alaska.

Checkered white and **cabbage white**: throughout the United States and the southern half of Canada.

Life Cycle

Whites overwinter as pupae. Depending on the season, the complete cycle from egg to butterfly can take from six to nine weeks. Most adults live between 6 to 10 days as butterflies.

When to Observe

Checkered and cabbage whites are among the first to appear in early spring, flying until fall in the North and year-round in the South; western whites usually appear from June to September.

How to Attract

• Plant flowering members of the mustard family, such as broccoli and cabbage, to serve as host plants.

• Plant nectar plants, including asters, clovers, chrysanthemums, hyssop, lavender, marigolds, mints, salvias, and zinnias; whites also obtain nutrients from mud puddles.

ZEBRAS

Zebra butterfly *(Heliconius charitonius)*

As a member of the longwing family of tropical butterflies (Heliconiidae), the zebra is unlike any other North American species. One of its unusual qualities is the zebra's ability to gather and consume pollen—the only butterfly known to do so. The pollen provides females the protein needed for continuous egg production and makes possible a relatively long adult life span of up to six months. Another unusual trait is that as the female is about to emerge from the chrysalis, she releases a scent that attracts a passing male. The male then mates with her. Consequently, females emerge from the chrysalis ready to lay eggs. Zebras have a somewhat distinct flight pattern: they exhibit slow and weak movements like a toddler learning to walk and drift about like a soap bubble floating through the air. Of course, that only makes them easy to follow and a delight to observe.

Description

ZEBRA *(Heliconius charitonius)*: elongated, intensely black wings, with the forewings twice as long as they are wide; wingspan measuring 3 to 3⅜ inches; trademark exotic blend of lemon yellow-striped patterns above,

with similar markings below in softer tones; several crimson spots at the base; the head emerges above the forewings as a well-shaped knob sitting on top of the thorax; a particularly long abdomen that extends as far back as the hindwings. The equally striking caterpillar is white with black spots and long black spines.

Range

Zebra: found in the United States throughout the year in the Deep South; occasionally strays beyond its normal range into the Southwest or north to the Great Plains.

Life Cycle

Unlike other butterflies that lay their eggs in masses on a variety of host plants, the female zebra lays only a few eggs at a time on a single passion vine plant. Since the zebra also obtains protein from pollen, she can live up to six months in order to lay a sufficient number of eggs. It takes only three weeks during warmer months for the butterfly to mature from an egg to an adult.

When to Observe

Zebras are active year-round in the South; appear from spring to early fall in northern regions.

How to Attract

• Plant passion vines to serve as host plants; they contain toxic chemicals that make both the caterpillar and adult butterfly distasteful to predators like birds.

• Plant a variety of trees, grasses, and flowers that provide pollen and/or nectar for adults, including passion vines, goldenrod, sunflowers, asters, willows, butterfly bushes, impatiens, lantanas, pentas, hyssop, and verbena.

Moth Profiles

Polyphemus (Antheraea polyphemus)

GIANT SILKS

The giant silk moth family (Saturniidae) features some of the largest and showiest moths in the world. Most of the 40 or so brightly colored species found in North America are creatures of the night, swooping through the air like bats, though the pink-and-yellow sheep moth (Hemileuca eglanterina), with its black striped accents, flies by day. Giant silk moths are, without doubt, quite spectacular.

Description

POLYPHEMUS (Antheraea polyphemus): striking and easily identifiable; named after Polyphemus (the one-eyed giant of Greek mythology) due to the transparent eyespots edged in yellow on each of its four wings; larger eyespots on the hindwings have additional blue and black rings; 3½- to 5½-inch-long velvety wings are yellow-orange to reddish brown, with a marginal line of smoky plum and white.

CECROPIA (Hyalophora cecropia): with a wingspan of up to six inches, it holds the title of North America's largest moth; bands of white and orange-red appear on both the wings and on its striped body; instead of eyespots, this species has four crescent-shaped white spots framed in orange-red, one on each wing.

IO (Automeris io): eye-catching; the 2½- to 3-inch wingspan is colored golden yellow on males and reddish to purplish brown on females; both sexes have reddish orange shading and marginal bands on the hindwings, with a strikingly prominent black eyespot that looks like a giant bull's-eye on each wing.

Range

Polyphemus: most widely distributed North American species, found throughout the United States and in southern Canada.

Cecropia and Io: generally found east of the U.S. Rockies and in southern Canada.

Life Cycle

The silk moth family has one or two broods a year, with moths generally on the wing in summer. Depending on the species, eggs can hatch in one to two weeks, with caterpillars taking six to eight weeks to mature. However, most species of giant silk moths overwinter as pupae, emerging as winged adults the following spring. Adults do not feed but spend their brief adult lives with the sole purpose of mating and laying eggs.

When to Observe

Polyphemus: from May to September.

Cecropia: from April to early July.

Io: July and August, with an earlier brood appearing in late April to May in the South.

How to Attract

• Will fly toward light.

• Plant a variety of broadleaf trees and shrubs to serve as host plants for laying eggs, and, later, as caterpillar food; plants especially sought after include alder, ash, birch, elm, maple, and oak as well as chestnut, hickory, apple, and cherry.

White-lined sphinx moth on verbena
(*Hyles lineata*)

SPHINX

Streamlined and swift best describe this group of stout-bodied moths, also known as hawk moths. With protruding heads, a large thorax, and wingspans for North American species ranging from 2 to 5½ inches, moths from the sphinx family (Sphingidae) are unmistakable. In fact, some day-flying species are easily mistaken for hummingbirds.

Description

CERISY'S or **ONE-EYED SPHINX** (*Smerinthus cerisyi*): wingspan of approximately 2½ to 3½ inches; wings marked by wavering bands of soft grays and browns; blue and black eyespots on the hindwings accented by rosy pink patches over tawny brown.

HUMMINGBIRD CLEARWING (*Hemaris thysbe*): wingspan of approximately 1½ to 2¼ inches, large, clear patches with a reddish brown border on both its forewings and hindwings; olive-colored body banded in wine red; hovers like a hummingbird while feeding during the day.

WHITE-LINED SPHINX (*Hyles lineata*): wingspan of approximately 2½ to 3½ inches; an intricate pattern of white stripes on brown forewings that are edged in buff; striking pink hindwings bordered by brown; fawn-colored body dotted with black-and-white bars.

Range

Cerisy's or **one-eyed sphinx**: west of the U.S. Rockies and throughout northern United States and Canada.

Hummingbird clearwing: common in Canada and the eastern United States.

White-lined sphinx: throughout North America, except for the far North.

Life Cycle

Most species overwinter as pupae underground, usually in a chamber in the soil. Some species craft a delicate cocoon at the soil surface that's hidden by organic debris.

When to Observe

Adults are generally out and about from May to October, depending on the species and region.

How to Attract

• Plant host plants for caterpillars: willows and cottonwoods for Cerisy's sphinx; members of the honeysuckle family for the hummingbird clearwing; and a variety of plants, from evening primrose, four o'clocks, and peonies to apples, pears, and grapes, for the white-lined sphinx.

• Plant nectar-rich, trumpet-shaped flowers for adults, such as petunias, foxglove, gladiolus, gladiolius and brugmansia.

Virgin tiger (*Grammia virgo*)

TIGERS

This group of small- to medium-sized moths has stocky bodies and broad wings, resulting in a slow and deliberate style of flight. Though some species of the tiger moth family (Arctiidae) are subtly patterned or colored, many display bright colors and boldly patterned wings that convey a jungle cat feel—hence the common name of "tiger" moth. Three widely distributed and especially striking species are listed below.

Description

ORNATE TIGER (*Apantesis ornata*): an average 1½ inch wingspan; intricate network of white veining and marginal lines over black on forewings; pink to red hindwings make a colorful backdrop for several black patches.

GARDEN TIGER (*Arctia caja*): may be quite variable in appearance, but generally distinguished by broad white bands over brown forewings and orange or yellow hindwings with several dark spots; orange abdomen with a series of black horizontal stripes.

VIRGIN TIGER (*Grammia virgo*): a 2- to 2¾-inch wingspan; distinctive pattern includes cream-colored veining and borders over black forewings; brightly colored orange-red hindwings; abdomen accented by black patches; occasionally, a less common yellow form also occurs.

Ornate tiger: typically resides in the western United States from the Great Basin to the Pacific Coast.

Garden tiger: throughout the northern United States and southern Canada.

Virgin tiger: east of the U.S. Rockies and into southeastern Canada, excluding Montana.

Life Cycle

Tiger moths produce from one generation a year in the far North to four generations a year in the South. Caterpillars spin silken cocoons and pupate, with the last generation of caterpillars overwintering before pupating. They then resume the cycle in spring.

When to Observe

Look for tiger moths anytime from spring to summer, depending on the species and region.

How to Attract

• Plant a wide variety of plant types, including native weeds and grasses, to serve as host plants: plant clovers and plantain for the virgin tiger and various flowering herbs for the ornate tiger.

• Plant a variety of flowering nectar plants—from purple coneflower and verbena to spirea and lilac—for adults.

• Most tiger moths are night fliers and therefore will fly toward light, though some species, like the garden tiger, can be spotted feeding on nectar by day.

Ilia *(Catocala ilia)*

UNDERWINGS

With approximately 100 species found in North America, underwings belong to the largest family of moths (Noctuidae), known as owlets. These brown or gray moths appear drab and nondescript when at rest, with only their forewings showing. The forewing pattern is often quite variable within the species, allowing underwings to blend in with native tree bark. But hidden beneath the forewings' camouflage pattern are brightly colored hindwings, some bearing striped bands of beautiful color. Unlike some moths whose antennae are feathery, underwings' antennae are slender and threadlike.

Description

ILIA *(Catocala ilia)*: a wingspan of just over 3 inches; speckled black and gray to mottled dark grayish brown forewings with uneven black lines; orange underwings with irregular cocoa brown bands.

SWEETHEART *(Catocala amatrix)*: a wingspan of just over 3 inches; bark-like pattern on forewings; pinkish-orange underwings with irregular bands of dark cocoa brown to black and a narrow band of cream-colored edging.

AHOLIBAH *(Catocala aholibah)*: a wingspan of just over 3 inches; bark-like camouflage pattern on forewings; orange-red hindwings with irregular cocoa brown bands and narrowly fringed in white.

LITTLE NYMPH

(Catocala micronympha): a wingspan measuring just under 1¾ inches; typical camouflage earth-tone patterns on forewings; yellow underwings highlighted by cocoa-colored stripes.

Range

Ilia: the eastern two-thirds of the United States and in southern Canada; one of the most widespread and abundant of the underwings.

Sweetheart: the eastern United States and southwest to Arizona as well as in southern Canada.

Aholibah: mostly in the western United States and then north into the southern portions of British Columbia.

Little nymph: in eastern North America.

Life Cycle

Both larvae and adult moths rest by day on tree trunks or limbs, though larvae can sometimes be found on the ground, hidden beneath organic debris. This group of moths spends the winter stage as eggs on the bark of trees.

Dragonfly & Damselfly Profiles

When to Observe

Underwings typically make their appearance from June to September, depending on the species and region.

How to Attract

• Plant trees such as walnut, oak, and hickory, along with aspens, poplars, cottonwoods, and willows to serve as host plants.

• Like all nocturnal moths, adult under-wings will fly toward light. In addition, they'll be attracted by moth bait paint-ed on tree trunks. The ingredients for moth bait vary, but they usually include a ripened or fermented slurry of stale beer, an overly ripe banana or two, and several tablespoons of molasses or sugar.

Familiar bluet damselfly *(Enallagma civile)*

ATTRACTING DRAGONFLIES & DAMSELFLIES

You can sum up how to go about attracting dragonflies and dam-selflies in one word: water. Carnivo-rous feeders, they need water to breed and reproduce. Wetland attractions, such as a backyard pond or bog, are the best way to invite these creatures to stay. Wetland plants are equally essential since many species lay their eggs within plant tissues. Underwater plants also provide immature dragonflies and damselflies, called nymphs or naiads, with places to hunt for prey and hide from predators like fish.

BLUETS

True to its name, most of the 35 species of bluets found in North America are primarily bright blue with black markings, though a few species are red, orange, or yellow. This family (Coenagrionidae) of 1- to 2-inch-long insects, also known as narrow-winged damselflies, is the largest group of damselflies.

Description

FAMILIAR BLUET
(Enallagma civile): averages slightly under 1½ inches in length; clear wings with black veining; males have a bright, sky blue thorax and abdomen with black markings; females are mostly black above and a pale blue or tan below and on the thorax.

NORTHERN BLUET
(Enallagma cyathigerum): averages slightly under 1½ inches in length; clear wings with black veining; males are bright turquoise blue from head to tail with scattered black markings; females greenish gold, pale blue, or brown.

ORANGE BLUET *(Enallagma signatum)*: averages slightly under 1½ inches in length; clear wings with black veining; orange from head to tail with black markings and yellow rings.

Range

Familiar bluet: most widespread; ranges across the United States, except for Washington and Idaho; also in southern Canada.

Northern bluet: most of North America, excluding the far North and the Southwest.

Orange bluet: the eastern United States.

When to Observe

Most adults emerge in early summer, with the northern bluet making its first appearance in late spring.

Where to Observe

Bluets frequent ponds but can also be found at lakes, marshes, and slow-moving streams and rivers. Males fly long distances over open waters and nearby uplands. Depending on the species, they may perch horizontally or obliquely on vegetation near the water's edge or on higher ground; some perch horizontally on the ground or on logs.

A tandem pair of spotted spreadwing damselflies *(Lestes congener)* just before or after mating

SPREADWINGS

These metallic-looking damselflies are larger than most damselflies, with a body ranging from 1¼ to 2 inches. Like other damselflies, spreadwings are delicate-looking creatures with slender, stalk-like bodies and widely separated, bulging eyes located on the sides of the head. You can distinguish this group from other damselflies by their relatively large size and by the way in which they hold their wings at rest: partially spread open rather than held parallel along the length of the body. Of the 10 species of spreadwings found in North America, the three most widespread are listed below.

Description

COMMON SPREADWING *(Lestes disjunctus)*: averages 1½ inches in length; blue eyes; males are deep bronze above with slender, pale yellow shoulder stripes; abdomen and tail tip dry-brushed in pale blue bands; females and immature males are tan to dull brown with thin bluish gray markings.

SPOTTED SPREADWING *(Lestes congener)*: averages 1½ inches in length; blue eyes; male coloring is similar to that of the common spreadwing, but more intense; females and immature males are tan to dull brown with bluish gray markings.

EMERALD SPREADWING *(Lestes dryas)*: averages 1½ inches in length; blue eyes; the stockiest of North American damselflies, though still fairly thin; most distinguishing characteristic is its color: metallic green above, blue face, and powdered blue tail tip; female is similar, but more muted in color.

Range

Common spreadwing: throughout North America, with the exception of the far North.

Spotted spreadwing: from coast to coast in North America, excluding the far North and most Gulf Coast states.

Emerald spreadwing: much of North America, excluding the far North, the South, and the Southeast.

When to Observe

Depending on the species and region, spreadwings make their appearance from early summer until fall, with southern forms emerging in spring.

Where to Observe

Ponds with vegetation along the shorelines are common hangouts, especially when wetland plantings include cattails, bulrushes, or sedges. Other wetland retreats generally include marsh-bordered lakes, marshes, and slow streams. Look for colorful males quietly perched obliquely on vegetation. They fly briefly, usually for short distances. Females only appear at wetland locations when ready to breed.

Blue dasher *(Pachydiplax longipennis)*

BLUE DASHER

Only an average of 1½ inches in length, this dragonfly's strong suit may not be size. The blue dasher (Pachydiplax longipennis) is often a familiar site around ponds. Watching males compete is like watching an aerial duel: they meet above the pond's surface with abdomens raised, each trying to outmaneuver the other until one eventually drives its opponent out of sight.

Description

BLUE DASHER

(Pachydiplax longipennis): mainly blue-bodied skimmer family member has conspicuous characteristics lacking in other blue-colored dragonflies: a waxy blue abdomen progressing from deeper shades of blue to nearly black on both ends; metallic blue-green eyes; a black-and-yellow striped thorax; amber to smoky brown wings; females are generally charcoal brown with amber-colored markings and shorter abdomens with a rounded tip.

Range

Blue dasher: abundant throughout most of the United States and the extreme southern portions of Canada.

When to Observe

This dashing blue dragonfly is most plentiful in summer—but generally appears in the north from summer to fall and from spring to fall in the southern areas of its range.

Where to Observe

While this species is likely to turn up at a variety of wetland habitats, it's frequently found at vegetative ponds. When males aren't patrolling the water surface and females aren't depositing eggs, they perch horizontally on slender stems near the shoreline or away from water—from ground level to high up in the trees.

Shadow darner dragonfly *(Aeshna umbrosa)*

DARNERS

Members of this family (Aeshnidae) are among the fastest and largest of dragonflies, with wingspans up to 6 inches, bodies ranging from 2½ to 5 inches in length, and have particularly huge eyes. Unlike most dragonflies, darners have long, slender abdomens that taper slightly just behind the thorax, a characteristic needlelike shape that inspired their name. Of the 39 darner species found in North America, 20 generally similar species belong to the mosaic group (Aeshna). Mosaic darners typically have long, amber-tinted wings and dark bodies with intricate spots in shades of blue, green, or yellow all over their abdomens, unlike other darner species who tend to have bold, solid, or nondescript markings. The females are duller in color, with markings usually ranging from brown and yellow to green. Mosaics generally average about 3 inches in length.

Description

SHADOW DARNER

(Aeshna umbrosa): the most widely distributed mosaic; dark brown dragonfly with dull green eyes, green markings on the thorax, and blue spots on the abdomen.

BLUE-EYED DARNER

(Aeshna multicolor): more striking in color than the shadow darner, with bright blue eyes and face, a striped thorax, and abdominal spots on a dark brown body.

VARIABLE DARNER

(Aeshna interrupta): two forms: a striped variation found in the central United States and Canada and a spotted form found in the Northeast and western United States; regardless of their shape, the blue spots are on brown bodies; greenish blue eyes.

Range

Shadow darner: throughout North America, except for the far North and the South.

Blue-eyed darner: the western two-thirds of the United States and then north into southern British Columbia.

Variable darner: most of North America, excluding the entire Southeast and far North.

When to Observe

The blue-eyed and variable darners appear from spring to fall, with peak numbers seen in July and August. The shadow darner appears spring through fall as well and is one of the species last dragonflies to fly in northern regions.

Where to Observe

You can find mosaics at a variety of wetlands, including vegetated ponds, lakes, and slow-moving streams. Look for them hanging vertically from vegetation, hovering close to the bank, or out over the water's surface; they are especially active when feeding over clearings just before dusk and dawn.

Autumn or yellow-legged meadowhawk *(Sympetrum vicinum)*

MEADOWHAWKS

They're mostly red and typically hunt for small prey in grassy meadows. Perhaps that's why this group of small- to medium-sized dragonflies is known both as meadowhawks and as red skimmers. If you catch sight of one, you've got a good chance of seeing it up close since they move and fly in low gear. Adults of these species are commonly 1¼ to 1½ inches long. Of the 13 North American species, three widespread standouts are listed below.

Description

WHITE-FACED MEADOWHAWK *(Sympetrum obtrusum)*: red with a reddish brown thorax and eyes; black triangles running down the sides of the abdomen; a characteristic white face; females are more yellow than red and mature to a dull olive color.

AUTUMN MEADOWHAWK *(Sympetrum vicinum)*: also known as the yellow-legged meadowhawk; a red face and abdomen; a chestnut red thorax and eyes; minimal or absent black markings; yellow legs seen during the imma-ture adult stage darken to brown with age; females are more yellow than red, with mature females changing to a reddish or muted brown.

VARIEGATED MEADOWHAWK *(Sympetrum corruptum)*: a mosaic of orange-to-red rings on the abdomen, with golden brown and grayish white patches; colors are lighter and more muted in females, with the pattern in males fading to mostly red with age.

Range

White-faced meadowhawk: throughout most of North America, except for the far North and the South.

Autumn meadowhawk: most of the United States and the southeast tip of Canada, though numbers are somewhat scattered in the West.

Variegated meadowhawk: throughout the United States and southern Canada, with migratory numbers in the spring and fall in the eastern part of Canada and the United States.

When to Observe

Species in the north arrive in summer to fall and are typically among the last dragonflies to emerge. Meadowhawks in the south appear spring to fall and occasionally year-round.

Where to Observe

Meadowhawks frequent a variety of wetland locations, including ponds, marshes, bogs, and slow streams. They also venture far from water to nearby backyard gardens. When not airborne or perching on vegetation, adults can be spotted perching on small branches, rocks, or on the ground. Like butterflies, they also bask in sunny areas on rocks and stones.

Widow skimmer dragonfly (*Libellula luctuosa*)

SKIMMERS

Frequently spotted at ponds, skimmers are arguably the most fascinating of all dragonflies to watch. For starters, members of this large family exhibit diverse colors, wing patterns, and habits. They perch horizontally, vertically, or obliquely on vegetation, tree trunks, rocks, or even on the ground. With bodies measuring up to 2½ inches long, these strong fliers aren't quite as large as darners. But what they lack in size, they more then make up for in assertiveness.

Description

TWELVE-SPOTTED SKIMMER (*Libellula pulchella*): brown eyes; abdomen dusted in powder blue; the wings have bold patterns common to all skimmers, 12 brown spots separated by chalky white spots.

EIGHT-SPOTTED SKIMMER (*Libellula forensis*): similar to the twelve-spot, with eight brown spots and clear or chalky white wingtips instead of brown.

WIDOW SKIMMER (*Libellula luctuosa*): boldly patterned wings, with broad, dark chocolate patches near the base and whitish markings in the middle.

SLATY SKIMMER (*Libellula incesta*): deep slate-blue body; black face and eyes; clear wings with a narrow band of black at the tips.

FLAME SKIMMER (*Libellula saturata*): males are a striking, saturated orange and red from head to toe, including red eyes and wing veins; averages 2 inches long; females are typically brown with yellow markings.

Range

Twelve-spotted skimmer: from coast to coast in the United States and southern Canada.

Eight-spotted skimmer: western United States.

Widow skimmer: most of the United States, except for the interior West from Utah and Nevada and then northward.

Slaty skimmer: the eastern United States.

Flame skimmer: the western half of the United States, with the exception of Washington and North Dakota.

When to Observe

Skimmers are most active in summer but can also be observed from spring to fall, depending on the species and region.

Where to Observe

Skimmers forage and perch in a variety of places—from ponds, lakes, slow streams, and sometimes even bogs to clearings, fields, meadows, and gardens, where they perch on lavender and other garden plants. What makes this group so easy to observe is their tendency to remain still, returning to the same spot between flights.

Appendix
A LIST OF COMMON &
SCIENTIFIC NAMES

lady banks rose

African daisy (*Osteospermum* spp.)
amaranth (*Amaranthus* spp.)
American arborvitae
    (*Thuja occidentalis*)
American elderberry
    (*Sambucus canadensis*)
American mountain ash
    (*Sorbus americana*)
amethyst flower (*Browallia* spp.)
amur honeysuckle (*Lonicera maackii*)
angels' trumpet (*Brugmansia* spp)
anise hyssop (*Agastache* spp.)
annual lupine (*Lupinus nanus*)
arrow-wood
    (*Viburnum dentatum*)
ash (*Fraxinus* spp.)
aspen (*Populus* spp.)
asters (*Aster* spp.)
astilbe (*Astilbe arendsii*)
autumn olive (*Elaeagnus umbellata*)

bachelor's buttons
    (*Centaurea cyanus*)
bacopa (*Sutera cordata*)
bay (*Persea* spp.)
beautyberry (*Callicarpa americana*)
beauty bush (*Kolkwitzia amabilis*)
bellflower (*Campanula* spp.)
birch (*Betula* spp.)
black chokeberry
    (*Aronia melanocarpa*)
black elder (*Sambucus nigra*)
black-eyed Susan (*Rudbeckia hirta, Rudbeckia fulgida*)
black haw (*Viburnum prunifolium*)
blanket flower (*Gaillardia* spp.)
bluebeard (*Caryopteris* spp.)
blue fescue (*Festuca glauca*)
blue oat grass (*Helictotrichon sempervirens*)
bog arum (*Calla palustris*)
borage (*Borago officinalis*)

Angels' trumpet or brugmansia

Boston ivy
    (*Parthenocissus tricuspidata*)
Bowles' golden sedge
    (*Carex elata* 'Aurea')
box elder (*Acer negundo*)
box honeysuckle (*Lonicera nitida*)
bridal wreath spirea
    (*Spiraea prunifolia*)
broom corn (*Panicum miliaceum*)
brugmansia (*Brugmansia* spp.)
bur oak (*Quercus macrocarpa*)
butterfly bush (*Buddleja* spp.)
butterfly flower (*Schizanthus* spp.)
butterfly weed (*Asclepias tuberosa*)

calendula (*Calendula* spp.)
California fuchsia (*Zauschneria* spp.)
candytuft (*Iberis* spp.)
caraway thyme
    (*Thymus herba-barona*)
cardinal flower (*Lobelia cardinalis*)
carpet bugle (*Ajuga* spp.)
catmint (*Nepeta* spp.)
cattails (*Typha* spp.)
chain ferns (*Woodwardia* spp.)
chameleon plant

    (*Houttuynia cordata*)
chaste tree (*Vitex agnus-castus*)
Chinese juniper (*Juniperus chinensis*)
cinnamon fern
    (*Osmunda cinnamonea*)
chrysanthemum
    (*Chrysanthemum* spp.)
clematis (*Clematis* spp.)
cleome (*Cleome hasslerana*)
climbing honeysuckle
    (*Lonicera* spp.)
climbing hydrangea
    (*Hydrangea anomala petiolaris*)
climbing rose (*Rosa* spp.)
Colorado blue spruce
    (*Picea pungens*)
columbine (*Aquilegia* spp.)
common calla lilly
    (*Zantedeschia aethiopica*)
common hops (*Humulus lupulus*)
common juniper
    (*Juniperus communis*)
common prickly ash
    (*Zanthoxylum americanum*)
coneflower (*Echinacea* spp.)
coral bells (*Heuchera* spp.)
coreopsis (*Coreopsis* spp.)
cosmos (*Cosmos bipinnatus*)
cotoneaster (*Cotoneaster* spp.)
cottonwood (*Populus* spp.)
crabapple (*Malus* spp.)
cranberry cotoneaster
    (*Cotoneaster apiculatus*)
creeping Jenny
    (*Lysimachia nummularia*)
creeping St. John's wort
    (*Hypericum calycinum*)
creeping phlox (*Phlox subulata*)
creeping thyme (*Thymus serpyllum*)
creeping zinnia
    (*Sanvitalia procumbens*)
crocosmia (*Crocosmia* spp.)

Fountain grass or pennisetum

dame's rocket (*Hesperis matronalis*)
daphne (*Daphne* spp.)
delphinium (*Delphinium* spp.)
dianthus (*Dianthus* spp.)
dogwood (*Cornus* spp.)
doublefile viburnum
(*Viburnum plicatum*
var. *tomentosum*)
downy hawthorn
(*Crataegus mollis*)
dwarf aster (*Aster* spp.)
dwarf Colorado blue spruce
(*Picea pungens*)
dwarf European viburnum
(*Viburnum opulus* 'Compactum')
dwarf hosta (*Hosta* spp.)
dwarf periwinkle (*Vinca minor*)
dwarf pine (*Pinus contorta*
or P. *thunbergii*)
dwarf river birch (*Betula nigra*)
dwarf sunflower (*Helianthus* spp.)
dwarf zinnia (*Zinnia* spp.)
elder (*Sambucus* spp.)
elderberry (*Sambucus* spp.)

elm (*Ulmus* spp.)
English holly (*Ilex aquifolium*)
European cranberry bush
(*Viburnum opulus*)
European mountain ash
(*Sorbus aucuparia*)
European privet (*Ligustrum vulgare*)
European red elder
(*Sambucus racemosa*)
European white birch
(*Betula pendula*)
evening-scented stock
(*Matthiola longipetala*)

February daphne
(*Daphne mezereum*)
firethorn (*Pyracantha* spp.)
floss flower
(*Ageratum houstonianum*)
flowering dogwood (*Cornus florida*)
flowering star clusters
(*Pentas lanceolata*)
flowering tobacco (*Nicotiana* spp.)
fountain grass (*Pennisetum* spp.)
foxglove (*Digitalis* spp.)
fragrant sumac (*Rhus aromatica*)

gayfeather (*Liatris spicata*)
gazania (*Gazania* spp.)
geranium (*Pelargonium* spp.)
giant bellflower (*Campanula latifolia*)
gladiolus (*Gladiolus* spp.)
globe amaranth
(*Gomphrena globosa*)
globe thistle (*Echinops* spp.)
goldenrod (*Solidago* spp.)
golden sedge (*Carex elata* 'Aurea')
ground cover juniper
(*Juniperus* spp.)
gunnera (*Gunnera* spp.)

hardy canna (*Thalia dealbata*)
hawthorn (*Crataegus* spp.)
hedge maple (*Acer campestre*)
heliotrope
(*Heliotropium arborescens*)
holly (*Ilex* spp.)
hollyhocks (*Alcea rosea*)
honeysuckle (*Lonicera* spp.)
hops (*Humulus* spp.)
hop tree (*Ptelea trifoliata*)
horsetail (*Equisetum* spp.)
hosta (*Hosta* spp.)
hummingbird mint (*Agastache* spp.)

impatiens (*Impatiens walleriana*)
indian mulberry (*Morus indica*)
iris (*Iris* spp.)
Irish juniper (*Juniperus communis*)
Italian aster (*Aster amellus*)
ivy (*Hedera* spp.)
ivy geranium
(*Pelargonium peltatum*)

Jack-in-the-pulpit
Arisaema triphyllum)
Jack pine (*Pinus banksiana*)
Japanese barberry
(*Berberis thunbergii*)
Japanese forest grass
(*Hakonechloa macra*)
Japanese painted fern
(*Athyrium nipponicum*)
Japanese silver grass
(*Miscanthus sinensis*)
Japanese spirea (*Spiraea japonica*)
Japanese white pine
(*Pinus parviflora*)
jasmine (*Jasminum* spp.)
Joe-pye weed
(*Eupatorium purpureum*)
Joseph's coat (*Amaranthus tricolor*)
juniper (*Juniperus* spp.)

kousa dogwood
　(*Cornus kousa*)

lady banks rose (*Rosa banksias*)
lady fern (*Athyrium filix-femina*)
lantana (*Lantana camara*,
　L. montevidensis)
lavelle hawthorn
　(*Crataegus lavellei*)
lavender (*Lavandula* spp.)
little bluestem
　(*Schizachyrium scoparium*)
love-lies-bleeding
　(*Amaranthus caudatus*)
low-growing sedum (*Sedum* spp.)

mallow (*Malva* spp.)
maple (*Acer* spp.)
marigolds (*Tagetes* spp.)
marsh betony (*Stachys palustris*)
marsh marigold (*Caltha palustris*)
meadowsweet or **false spiraea**
　(*Astilbe* spp.)
meadowsweet (*Filipendula* spp.)
milkflower cotoneaster
　(*Cotoneaster lacteus*)
milkweed (*Asclepias* spp.)
milky bellflower
　(*Campanula lactiflora*)
monkey flower (*Mimulus* spp.)
moonbeam coreopsis
　(*Coreopsis verticillata*)
moonflower vine (*Ipomoea alba*)
moor grass (*Molinia* spp.)
morning glory (*Ipomoea* spp.)
moss phlox (*Phlox subulata*)
mother of thyme
　(*Thymus serpyllum*)

narrow-leafed firethorn
　(*Pyracantha angustifolia*)
nasturtium (*Tropaeolum majus*,
　T. peregrinum)
New England aster
　(*Aster novae-angliae*)
New Zealand hair sedge
　(*Carex comens*)
Norway maple
　(*Acer platanoides*)

oak (*Quercus* spp.)
orange butterfly bush
　(*Buddleja globosa*)
ornamental millet 'Purple Majesty'
　(*Pennisetum glaucum* 'Purple
　Majesty')

Pacific dogwood (*Cornus nuttallii*)
pagoda dogwood
　(*Cornus alternifolia*)
paperbark maple (*Acer griseum*)
parney cotoneaster (*Cotoneaster
　lacteus*)
parrot's beak (*Lotus berthelotii*)
passionflower (*Passiflora* spp.)
passion vine plant (*Passiflora* spp.)
pawpaw (*Asimina triloba*)
pearly everlasting
　(*Anaphalis margaritacea*)
pencil cedar (*Juniperus virginiana*)
pennisetum (*Pennisetum* spp.)
penstemon (*Penstemon* spp.)
petunia (*Petunia* spp.)
pincushion flower
　(*Scabiosa columbaria*)
pine (*Pinus* spp.)
poplar (*Populus* spp.)
potato vine (*Solanum crispum*)
prostrate rosemary

Pine

　(*Rosmarinus officinalis*)
purple amaranth
　(*Amaranthus cruentus*)
purple coneflower
　(*Echinacea purpurea*)
pussytoes (*Antennaria* spp.)
pussy willow (*Salix discolor*)

ramanas rose (*Rosa rugosa*)
red chokeberry (*Aronia arbutifolia*)
red elderberry (*Sambucus racemosa*)
moss phlox (*Phlox subulata*)
redleaf rose (*Rosa glauca*)
red maple (*Acer rubrum*)
red mulberry (*Morus rubra*)
red oak (*Quercus rubra*)
red osier dogwood
　(*Cornus stolonifera*)
river birch (*Betula nigra*)
rockspray cotoneaster
　(*Cotoneaster horizontalis*)
rose (*Rosa* spp.)
rose moss (*Portulaca grandiflora*)

Lantana

royal fern (*Osmunda regalis*)
rue (*Ruta graveolens*)
rugosa rose (*Rosa rugosa*)
rush (*Juncus* spp.)

sawtooth oak (*Quercus acutissima*)
scaevola (*Scaevola* spp.)
scarlet firethorn
    (*Pyracantha coccinea*)
scarlet monkeyflower
    (*Mimulus cardinalis*)
scarlet oak (*Quercus coccinea*)
scented geranium (*Pelargonium* spp.)
Scotch broom (*Cytisus scoparius*)
Scotch moss (*Sagina subulata*)
sea pink (*Armeria* spp.)
sedum, October daphne
    (*Sedum sieboldii*)
sedum (*Sedum* spp.)
senna (*Cassia* spp.)
showy sedum (*Sedum spectabile*)
Siberian crabapple (*Malus baccata*)
Siberian elm (*Ulmus pumila*)
silver maple (*Acer saccharinum*)
sky lupines (*Lupinus nanus*)
snapdragon (*Antirrhinum majus*)
southern crabapple
    (*Malus angustifolia*)
speedwell (*Veronica* spp.)
spicebush (*Lindera benzoin*)
spiderwort (*Tradescantia virginiana*)
spirea (*Spiraea* spp.)
spruce (*Picea* spp.)
summer phlox (*Phlox paniculata*)
sunflowers (*Helianthus annuus*)

swamp milkweed
    (*Asclepias incarnata*)
swamp white oak (*Quercus bicolor*)
sweet alyssum (*Lobularia maritima*)
sweet everlasting
    (*Gnaphalium obtusifolium*)
sweet flag (*Acorus* spp.)
switch grass (*Panicum virgatum*)

tansy ragwort (*Senecio jacobaea*)
tartarian honeysuckle
    (*Lonicera tatarica*)
thread leaf coreopsis
    (*Coreopsis verticillata*)
trailing periwinkle (*Vinca minor*)
trailing petunias (*Petunia* x *hybrida*)
trident maple (*Acer buergeranum*)
turtlehead (*Chelone lyonii*)

verbena (*Verbena* spp.)
vetch (*Vicia* spp.)
viburnum (*Viburnum* spp.)
violets (*Viola* spp.)
Virginia creeper
    (*Parthenocissus quinquefolia*)
Virginia pine (*Pinus virginiana*)

wallflower (*Erysimum cheiri*)
water birch (*Betula occidentalis*)
water hibiscus
    (*Hibiscus moscheutos palustris*)
water parsnip (*Sium suave*)
water plantain
    (*Alisma plantago-aquatica*)
weeping Canada hemlock

    (*Tsuga canadensis*)
weeping Colorado blue spruce
    (*Picea pungens* 'Procumbens')
weeping eastern white pine
    (*Pinus strobus* 'Pendulous')
weeping Japanese red pine
    (*Pinus densiflora* 'Pendula')
weeping Norway spruce
    (*Picea abies* 'Pendula')
weeping pussy willow
    (*Salix caprea* 'Pendula')
weeping willow (*Salix babylonica*)
white mulberry (*Morus alba*)
white oak (*Quercus alba*)
white spruce (*Picea glauca*)
willow (*Salix* spp.)
winterberry (*Ilex verticillata*)
wintercreeper (*Euonymus fortunei*)
winter honeysuckle
    (*Lonicera fragrantissima*)
witch hazel (*Hamamelis* spp.)
woolly thyme
    (*Thymus pseudolanuginosus*)
woolly yarrow (*Achillea tomentosa*)

yaupon holly (*Ilex vomitoria*)

zinnias (*Zinnia* spp.)

Acknowledgments

Dr. Karen Oberhauser, research associate at the University of Minnesota Department of Ecology, Evolution and Behavior; St. Paul, Minnesota (Monarch butterfly specialist); Dr. Stephen Malcolm, Deptartment of Biological Sciences at Western Michigan University (Monarch butterfly specialist); Lynn Royce, (Insect Identification Specialist) Plant Clinic, Botany and Plant Pathology at the Oregon State University in Corvallis, Oregon; Carol Beckley at Oregon's Butterfly Pavilion and education center in Elkton for letting us photograph her butterflies and garden. Thanks to the following photographers for sharing their gorgeous work with us: Ron Austing, Scott Bauer, Glenn Corbiere, Paul Opler, and D. Lynn Scott. And of course, the following people at Lark Books who assisted me with putting the book together: Terry Krautwurst for getting the ball rolling and Jane Woodside for her vision; Valerie Shrader for her project input and editing; and Deborah Morgenthal for her artistic direction. Thank you to everyone at Lark for their creativity, time, and effort in putting this book together.

USGS resources used in preparing wildlife profiles. Must be credited this way.

Ferguson, Douglas C., Chuck E. Harp, Paul A. Opler, Richard S. Peigler, Michael Pogue, Jerry A. Powell, and Michael J. Smith. 1999. *Moths of North America.* Jamestown, ND: Northern Prairie Wildlife Research Center Home Page.
http://www.npwrc.usgs.gov/resource/distr/lepid/moths/mothsusa. htm (Version 12DEC2003).

Igl, Lawrence D. 1996. *Bird Checklists of the United States.* Jamestown, ND: Northern Prairie Wildlife Research Center Online.
http://www.npwrc.usgs.gov/resource/birds/chekbird/chekbird.htm (Version 12MAY03).

Kondratieff, Boris C. (coordinator). 2000. *Dragonflies and Damselflies (Odonata) of the United States.* Jamestown, ND: Northern Prairie Wildlife Research Center Online.
http://www.npwrc.usgs.gov/resource/distr/insects/dfly/dflyusa.htm (Version 12DEC2003).

Opler, Paul A., Harry Pavulaan, and Ray E. Stanford (coordinators). 1995. *Butterflies of North America.* Jamestown, ND: Northern Prairie Wildlife Research Center Home Page.
http://www.npwrc.usgs.gov/resource/distr/lepid/bflyusa/bflyusa.htm (Version 12DEC2003).

Contributing Designers

Joan K. Morris' artistic endeavors have led her down many successful creative paths. A childhood interest in sewing turned into a career in professional costuming for motion pictures. After studying ceramics, Joan ran her own clay wind chime business. Since 1993, Joan's Asheville, North Carolina, coffee house, Vincent's Ear, has provided a vital meeting place for all varieties of artists and thinkers. Projects designed by Joan have been featured in a variety of Lark books.

George Harrison is a custom furniture maker who lives in Weaverville, North Carolina. Lark Books frequently calls on him to help with project construction.

Diana Light has an uncanny ability to make everything she touches look instantly cool. After earning her B.F.A. in painting and printmaking, Diana extended her expertise to etching and painting fine glass objects. She has contributed to numerous Lark books and lives and works in the beautiful Blue Ridge Mountains of North Carolina.

Additional design work contributed by:
George Harrison on the Hanging Platform Feeder, Nesting Materials Box, Robin Nest Shelf, Pitched Roof Nest Box, Chickadee Winter Roost Box, Woodpecker Box, and Orchard Mason Bee Box.

Diana Light on the Covered Bridge Fruit Feeder, Hanging Platform Feeder, Hummingbird Feeder, Pitched Roof Nest Box, Chickadee Winter Roost Box, Woodpecker House, and the Dragonfly Perch.

Susan McBride on the Butterfly Fruit Feeder, Orchard Mason Bee Box, and the Flowerpot Birdbath.

Joan K. Morris on the Wedge Nest Box, Screech Owl Box, and Hanging Bamboo Birdbath.

About the Author & the Photographer

Writer **Kris Wetherbee** and her photographer husband, Rick, live on a 40-acre farm in the hills of western Oregon. Kris is an expert organic gardener and wildlife enthusiast, who writes frequently in the areas of food, gardening, nature, and outdoor living. She has published in magazines such as *Sunset*, *Sierra, Audubon*, *Town & Country*, *Cooking Light*, *Woman's Day*, *Country Living*, and *Spa*.

Rick Wetherbee is a nationally known photographer who specializes in horticulture, wildlife, outdoor living, and food. His photographs have appeared in many of the same publications as his wife's work, as well as in others such as *Horticulture*, *Mother Earth News*, *European Homes & Gardens*, *Northwest Palate*, and *Organic Gardening*.

Metric Conversion Chart

INCHES TO MILLIMETERS & CENTIMETERS

Inches	Mm	Cm	Inches	Cm	Inches	Cm
⅛	3	0.3	9	22.9	30	76.2
¼	6	0.6	10	25.4	31	78.7
⅜	10	1.0	11	27.9	32	81.3
½	13	1.3	12	30.5	33	83.8
⅝	16	1.6	13	33.0	34	86.4
¾	19	1.9	14	35.6	35	88.9
⅞	22	2.2	15	38.1	36	91.4
1	25	2.5	16	40.6	37	94.0
1¼	32	3.2	17	43.2	38	96.5
1½	38	3.8	18	45.7	39	99.1
1¾	44	4.4	19	48.3	40	101.6
2	51	5.1	20	50.8	41	104.1
2½	64	6.4	21	53.3	42	106.7
3	76	7.6	22	55.9	43	109.2
3½	89	8.9	23	58.4	44	111.8
4	102	10.2	24	61.0	45	114.3
4½	114	11.4	25	63.5	46	116.8
5	127	12.7	26	66.0	47	119.4
6	152	15.2	27	68.6	48	121.9
7	178	17.8	28	71.1	49	124.5
8	203	20.3	29	73.7	50	127.0

Index